Ancient Egypt

Ancient Egypt

CAMPBELL PRICE

 Thames & Hudson

Contents

Introduction

Ancient Egypt ranks second only to dinosaurs in terms of its popularity in museums. Exhibitions on Egyptological subjects are common and museums regularly feature Egypt-themed objects in their gift shops even if they hold very few Egyptian objects or none at all. For many people, museums are synonymous with the idea of ancient Egypt. But why? Perhaps the material culture of pharaonic Egypt appeals to us because of its familiarity. While ancient Greek and Roman objects tend to be conflated in the popular imagination, ancient Egypt stands apart because of its distinctive visual markers. Unlike the products of Mesoamerican or European archaeology, Egyptian objects are usually familiar to schoolchildren and adults alike. This is, of course, due to the prominence of ancient Egypt in modern popular culture, yet it also says something important about the nature of the ancient objects themselves.

Due to a pervading sense of artistic decorum in ancient Egypt, artisans produced objects that drew upon the same visual language in an effort to make them look 'right'. Once the rules were laid down in the early Dynastic period, representations of many common motifs were largely fixed throughout the next three millennia. The Egyptian high-cultural tendency to copy or take inspiration from older works also ensured the consistency of concepts and imagery from the earliest kings down to the Roman emperors. This extraordinary cultural continuity – expressed through a similarity of forms and object types – may imply an extreme cultural conservatism. Yet Egyptian art can be anything but conservative, and was able to adapt both to innovations from within Egypt and to influences from outside its borders. The art of the Amarna period, for example, or Persian- or Roman-inspired funerary motifs show the vibrancy of artistic production. It is therefore better to speak of the confidence of pharaonic Egyptian art, from the smallest object to the largest monument, than of its conservatism.

For all of these reasons, ancient Egypt is highly collectable. Egyptian objects have taken a variety of routes to museums, none of which are predictable. From the late 1700s CE, ancient Egypt appeared like a mirage on the horizon of European thinking. Pharaonic Egypt had been familiar to Arabic scholarship for centuries before then, and was also mentioned in classical and biblical sources. Napoleon's expedition of 1798–1801 placed Egypt in a European political context, and the resulting folio volumes of the *Description de L'Egypte* (1809–29) are often cited as the starting point of Western study and collecting on a large scale. Governments and private individuals jostled for the best prizes – sometimes with official permits, sometimes without them – but rarely recorded the precise findspots of objects. What was once an occasional addition to a cabinet of curiosities became a huge acquisition industry filling private homes and national museums. Along the way, collectors and connoisseurs did irreparable damage in their quest to know 'ancient Egypt'.

Archaeological excavation is often praised as being objective and scientific, although often it has not met either of these aims. Archaeologists working in Egypt made deliberate selections of the areas and types of sites they wished to excavate: areas with ease of access and a willing local workforce. Archaeological practices on-site could be haphazard. Between 1880 and 1980, the Egyptian government permitted a proportion of archaeological finds to leave the country with their excavators. Due to this practice of division of finds – the so-called 'partage' system – in Egypt, certain sites (usually cemeteries or temples) were targeted by archaeologists in the hope of the richest rewards for their financial backers. Even then, some objects were particularly valued for export, some were damaged and some were even destroyed.

Once in the museum, academic and aesthetic considerations govern what is selected for research or display. Curators attempt to fit objects into an encompassing narrative of their own choosing, even if the objects in question come from very different contexts. Ancient Egypt covers such a vast span of time and geographical area that it is often easy to simplify and essentialize. The surviving evidence is biased even before it reaches an archaeologist or collector. Very little of settlements survives, due to the changing course of the River Nile gradually destroying most remains of ancient habitation, or modern cities being located right on top of ancient levels. What does survive tends to come from tombs located on the desert edge. Objects placed within them – posthumously by the living relatives

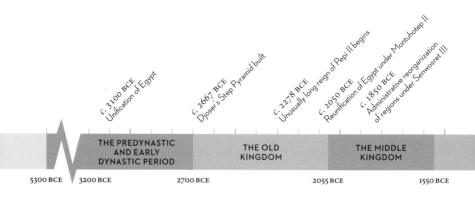

c. 3100 BCE
Unification of Egypt

c. 2667 BCE
Djoser's Step Pyramid built

c. 2278 BCE
Unusually long reign of Pepi II begins

c. 2050 BCE
Reunification of Egypt under Montuhotep II

c. 1850 BCE
Administrative reorganization
of regions under Senwosret III

THE PREDYNASTIC
AND EARLY
DYNASTIC PERIOD

THE OLD
KINGDOM

THE MIDDLE
KINGDOM

5300 BCE   3200 BCE   2700 BCE   2055 BCE   1550 BCE

rather the dead themselves – were included for various ritual reasons. Even if they have survived the widespread depredations of tomb robbery and time, these items belong almost exclusively to the wealthy. Ancient Egypt was a deeply unequal society, with access to high-cultural products restricted to few people. Monuments and mummification were expensive, and most of our evidence perpetuates elite ideals. We are therefore faced with a double bias: the contents of most museums significantly over-represent both death and the wealthiest members of society.

Bearing these caveats in mind, this book attempts to characterize some features of ancient Egyptian civilization through almost 200 objects, presented in seven chronological chapters. Within these chapters, objects have been arranged loosely chronologically and grouped according to themes – items of household use or adornment, objects relating to the state and the pharaoh, items associated with religious practice, and those connected with death and the afterlife. Due to the nature of the ancient Egyptian worldview, these categories were not distinct and the same object might sit in two or three different categories at once.

These atypically well-preserved pieces provide a remarkable, if fleeting, glimpse into a world very different from our own but which may yet seem familiar to us. Inevitably, the story the ancient Egyptians would have themselves wished to tell is that presented in monumental contexts. The presence of many works of sculpture in part reflects my own interests but also the cultural importance of these forms of presentation. Metal items are exceptional because of their susceptibility to reuse, while perishable organic objects give an insight into items many 'ordinary' Egyptians would have used on a day-to-day basis. Each of these objects offers a privileged, if partial, view of the experience of being an ancient Egyptian.

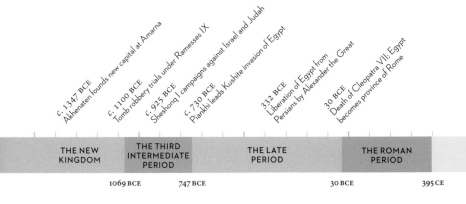

c. 1347 BCE
Akhenaten founds new capital at Amarna

c. 1100 BCE
Tomb robbery trials under Ramesses IX

c. 925 BCE
Sheshonq I campaigns against Israel and Judah

c. 730 BCE
Piankhi leads Kushite invasion of Egypt

332 BCE
Liberation of Egypt from Persians by Alexander the Great

30 BCE
Death of Cleopatra VII; Egypt becomes province of Rome

THE NEW KINGDOM	THE THIRD INTERMEDIATE PERIOD	THE LATE PERIOD	THE ROMAN PERIOD
	1069 BCE	747 BCE	30 BCE	395 CE

MAP OF ANCIENT EGYPT

Egypt is in the north east of Africa and
is dominated by the River Nile, which
cuts through an otherwise largely desert
landscape northwards towards the
Mediterranean. The influence of Egyptian
culture stretched far beyond its own
borders in ancient times as today.

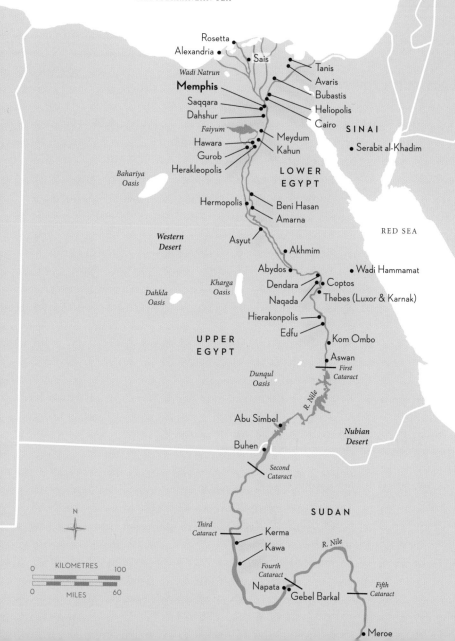

MEDITERRANEAN SEA

Rosetta
Alexandria
Sais
Tanis
Avaris
Bubastis
Memphis
Heliopolis
Saqqara
Cairo
Dahshur
Wadi Natrun
Faiyum
SINAI
Meydum
Hawara
Kahun
Gurob
Serabit al-Khadim
Herakleopolis
*Bahariya
Oasis*
LOWER
EGYPT
Hermopolis
Beni Hasan
Amarna
*Western
Desert*
Asyut
RED SEA
Akhmim
Abydos
Wadi Hammamat
*Kharga
Oasis*
Dendara
Coptos
*Dahkla
Oasis*
Naqada
Thebes (Luxor & Karnak)
Hierakonpolis
Edfu
UPPER
EGYPT
Kom Ombo
Aswan
*First
Cataract*
*Dunqul
Oasis*
R. Nile
Abu Simbel
*Nubian
Desert*
Buhen
*Second
Cataract*
SUDAN
*Third
Cataract*
Kerma
Kawa
R. Nile
*Fourth
Cataract*
N
Napata
Gebel Barkal
*Fifth
Cataract*
0 KILOMETRES 100
0 MILES 60
Meroe

Egypt at its Origins

Among the first preserved statues unequivocally depicting the pharaoh, this image of Khasekhemwy was reconstructed from fragments. He wears the white crown of Upper Egypt and the robe associated with the 'heb-sed' or royal jubilee festival. The base of the statue is etched with details of 47,209 slain enemies, apparently of Lower Egyptian origin.

By about 4500 BCE, climatic change in north-eastern Africa resulted in gradual population shifts. Drier conditions obliged Neolithic foragers and big-game hunters to settle next to the River Nile as the desert became more inhospitable. The Nile provided a unifying artery, or backbone, for a nascent state.

The Egyptians of the Predynastic period developed a variety of means to exploit resources, both within Egypt and further afield. Worked semi-precious stones and shells from coastlines attest to significant trading contacts exploited in pursuit of personal adornment. Among the most important developments were advances in stoneworking. Using simple copper and flint tools with sand as an abrasive, this technology enabled the sculpting of monumental, polished stone vessels. In fact, the hieroglyphic word for 'craft' is written with the sign for a bow drill of the type used in the labour-intensive production of such vessels, demonstrating its early cultural importance and acting as a precursor for later pharaonic monumentalism.

Interpretation of the Predynastic period, more than any other, is dominated by a large number of burial sites that have been extensively excavated, rather than settlements. Predynastic burials are simple by later, elite standards, with the corpse crouched in a foetal position, covered in skins or matting and laid in a shallow pit. The desiccating action of the desert sand often preserved the corpse naturally. It is unclear if observation of this phenomenon was a determining factor in the later development of artificial mummification, as is often stated. Perhaps more likely, social changes motivated the more elaborate ritual display surrounding death; wrapping and anointing of the body may therefore not have been aimed at preserving the corpse.

Grave objects imply that expectations for the afterlife were already present and that the items were chosen to exhibit forms of social differentiation. Jewelry was commonly included, as were flat greywacke palettes used for crushing pigment for cosmetics. Pottery vessels imply the capacity to eat and drink in, or on the journey to, an existence after death. The inclusion of weapons, in the form of mace heads, may be markers of social status or suggest that defence was thought necessary in, or on the way into, the afterlife.

When the British archaeologist William Matthew Flinders Petrie (1853–1942) located thousands of Predynastic graves at Naqada in southern Egypt he assumed that they belonged to a 'New Race' of invaders, because the material culture found with the burials seemed to him so alien. Eventually Petrie conceded his surmise to be incorrect, but his initial theory has had significant repercussions and his relative 'sequence dating' of pottery is still generally valid.

The Predynastic period is essentially silent in terms of written sources because those 'texts' that survive are short, staccato captions and labels from the end of the period. Continuous texts did not appear for several centuries. Rather, the Predynastic worldview is articulated and interpreted mostly through figural images. Repeated motifs imitate the riverine landscape of Egypt: water, boats, plants, animals, humans. The most common medium for such imagery is pottery. Although not immediately recognizable as 'Egyptian' to most non-specialists today, these nascent

Royal names were key markers of royal identity. This stone stela carries only the royal name – that of King Djet – framed within a serekh *or 'palace facade' motif. Atop the palace perches a majestic falcon – a representation of the god Horus, who was closely associated with the pharaoh.*

forms eventually led to the establishment of key elements of pharaonic visual culture.

The eventual unification of Egypt about 3100 BCE into a single 'nation' state – although that term is anachronistic – was more gradual than the Narmer ceremonial palette (see p.28) would suggest. Of greatest importance for the Egyptian sense of self was the figure of the king. Government, such as it was, centred on the royal palace and consisted of the small number of individuals closest to the ruler. It is significant that the development of monumental hieroglyphs seems to originate with the royal name, which began to be written inside a frame imitating distinctive palace architecture. The ruler and the palace were in some sense synonymous.

At the royal cemetery of Abydos, Egypt's first kings – one of whom, Merneith, seems to have been a woman – are identifiable through commodities labelled with inscriptions of their names. Later Egyptians would blend history and myth, and identify the tomb of the god Osiris himself amid this necropolis. The sacred part of Abydos known as Umm el-Qaab (Arabic for 'Mother of Pots', after pilgrims' offerings for Osiris) was, therefore, the birthplace of kingship in Egypt.

Abydos is strewn with potsherds, left by countless pilgrims bringing offerings to the god Osiris. As the necropolis of the earliest kings of the united 'Two Lands', Abydos was one of Egypt's most sacred places of pilgrimage. The historical memory of these early rulers blurred with the mythology of Osiris.

Pleated garment

c. 3482 – 3102 BCE
Linen • Height: 58 cm (22¾ in.) • From Tarkhan, Egypt
PETRIE MUSEUM OF EGYPTIAN ARCHAEOLOGY,
LONDON, UK

The remarkable survival of organic material in Egypt,
even delicate items such as linen clothing, offers
insights about life that may not be depicted in other
sources. This V-necked, partly pleated garment is
the world's oldest known woven item of clothing.
It was stitched together from three separate pieces
of handwoven fabric. Creases under the arms and
at the elbows indicate real-life use. As clothing was
expensive, it was common for garments to be reused
for preparing the dead. Only in 2015 were reliable
tests carried out to reveal that the garment is several
centuries older than previously thought.

HIPPO BOWL

c. 3500 BCE
Pottery with white hand-painted decoration • Diameter: 23 cm (9 in.)
From El-Mahasna, Egypt

MANCHESTER MUSEUM, UK

Despite its 'cute' appeal to modern sensibilities, the hippopotamus
is still one of the most dangerous large animals in Africa.
Hippos often represented chaos for the Egyptians, so the image
of them encircling this bowl may be intended to represent
control over nature. This harnessing of the power of dangerous
entities became typical of later Egyptian material culture.
Pharaonic representations of the hippo – notably in the form
of the protective mother goddess Taweret – focus on the
animal's fearsomeness and fecundity. These characteristics
were harnessed to protect pregnant women and children.
It is hard to say if these associations were intended during
the Predynastic period, when the bowl was made.

The bowl may have once contained food offerings
for the afterlife, and also represented eternally
replenished sustenance in the grave. The grave
in which it was found contained carved hippo
tusks, and it is intriguing to speculate why its
owner was so well equipped with power from hippo
symbolism – perhaps the person buried in the grave
was an otherwise unattested ritual or healing practitioner.

*Hippos fighting on the River
Nile, in modern-day Sudan.
The ancient Egyptians
described the aggressive
cries of hippopotamuses
as being audible from
hundreds of miles away.*

Vessel painted with landscape

c. 3400 BCE

Pottery with red painted decoration
Height: 32 cm (12 ⅝ in.), diameter:
28 cm (11 in.) • *From Egypt*

MANCHESTER MUSEUM, UK

Pottery vessels with bold, simple decoration of this type may not at first appear particularly pharaonic. They are in fact characteristic of Predynastic Egyptian art and are so appealing that they are often faked. Much discussion pertains to their meaning and symbolism. The highly stylized scenes appear to reference features of the landscape. The most common motifs are long-necked birds as seen here, which may be ostriches or flamingos, depictions of boats with oars, and triangles to represent hills or mountains. Where human figures appear that may imply a ritual rather than an everyday setting. The small projecting handles just below the rim of the vessel are pierces for suspension.

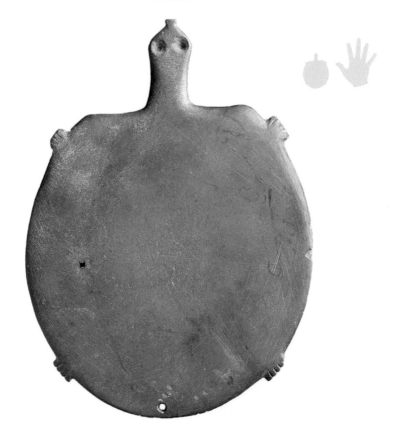

Turtle-shaped cosmetic palette

c. 3500 BCE
Greywacke • Height: 13.8 cm (5 ⅜ in.), width: 10.2 cm (4 in.) • Most likely from Naqada, Egypt

MUSEUM OF FINE ARTS, BOSTON, USA

Eye make-up was worn by both men and women in ancient Egypt. This flat stone palette provided an ideal surface for crushing pigments – such as malachite or lead galena – for application around the eyes. This had antibacterial properties as well as reducing glare from the sun. Cosmetic palettes were a popular item in Predynastic graves and indicate the importance of physical appearance to the Egyptians. Many of the palettes take the shape of animals such as turtles or birds. Although the symbolism of animals is not clear at this early point in Egypt, turtles must have been common along the River Nile.

Cosmetic palette with Christian inscription

c. 3500 BCE

Greywacke • Height: 33.7 cm (13 ¼ in.), width: 10.2 cm (4 in.) • From Egypt

MICHAEL C. CARLOS MUSEUM, ATLANTA, USA

Rarely do objects from Egypt represent such a timespan between creation and eventual reuse. The original purpose of this object was as a surface on which to grind pigment for make-up, *c.* 3500 BCE. The same properties that made this smooth, flat stone palette suited to grinding make-up later made it ideal to carry an inscription. While ancient Egyptians often added to or reused writing surfaces, the gap in usage here is about 4,000 years. The inscription, beneath identifiable cross shapes, is an indecipherable Gnostic text. Gnosticism was an esoteric form of early Christianity practised in Egypt during the 1st century CE.

String of valuable coloured beads

c. 4200 – 3300 BCE
Carnelian, quartz, glazed steatite,
lapis • Length: 11.5 cm (4 ½ in.)
From Mesaid, Egypt

MUSEUM OF FINE ARTS, BOSTON, USA

Adornment of the body was a competitive pursuit in ancient Egyptian culture. Those with sufficient wealth and access to resources were able to commission high-status, ostentatious objects. These beads would have been strung to wear around the neck, wrist or ankle, and represent the end product of an extensive network of mining and trade. While quartz and glazed steatite could be sourced within Egypt, rich red carnelian and bright blue lapis had to be brought from distant lands. The symbolism of the stones for both the living and the dead was matched by the attractiveness of their colours.

Model of a building

c. 3200 BCE

*Pottery • Height: 24.2 cm (9 ½ in.), width: 26.7 cm (10 ½ in.),
length: 38 cm (15 in.) • From El-Amra, Egypt*

BRITISH MUSEUM, LONDON, UK

Due to the nature of archaeological preservation in Egypt,
little survives of mud-brick buildings in contrast to stone-built
tombs and temples. There is a lack of remaining structures of
perishable materials in the floodplain, where most people
chose to live – and still do. As a consequence, models like
this are a useful indication of how buildings once appeared.
The nature of this roofed structure is not clear. It appears to
have been mud-brick, with doorway and window frames
made from timber. The purpose of the model may have
been to provide an alternative home for the spirit of the
deceased, similar to later so-called 'soul houses'.

Lion-shaped gaming piece

c. 3000 BCE

Ivory • Height: 3 cm (1 ⅛ in.),
width: 2 cm (¾ in.), length: 5.7 cm
(2 ¼ in.) • From Abydos, Egypt

ORIENTAL INSTITUTE,
CHICAGO, USA

While lions represented kingly and divine majesty, they could also appear in more domestic contexts. This finely carved ivory piece is a small sculpture in its own right and was found with several others. These appear to have been used as gaming pieces. A depiction of such objects alongside a 'gaming board' appears in the slightly later tomb of Hesire at Saqqara. This suggests that pieces were laid out on a board, in the manner of a modern game of draughts. The inclusion of gaming pieces in tombs implies a ritual significance, rather than simply a pastime in the afterlife.

Oversized stone vessel

c. 3200 BCE
Porphyry • Height: 56.5 cm (22 ¼ in.),
diameter: 61.5 cm (24 ¼ in.)
From Hierakonpolis, Egypt

MANCHESTER MUSEUM, UK

Ancient Egyptian monuments usually take the form of stone statues or stelae, but monumental hardstone vessels were an important way of emphasizing status during the Predynastic and early Dynastic periods. Stoneworking had developed in Egypt over centuries, and techniques had become refined. Large vessels such as this involved a conspicuous consumption of labour and would have taken several months to carve with a bow drill of flint, using sand as an abrasive. The resulting stone vessel has two lug handles, although it is unlikely these were used as the object was not suited to being transported. This impracticality indicates the vessel was used in a ritual context in a temple.

Scorpion mace head

c. 3100 BCE

Limestone • Height: 25 cm (9 ⅞ in.)
From Hierakonpolis, Egypt

ASHMOLEAN MUSEUM,
OXFORD, UK

The origins of Egyptian kingship extend back before the country's unification. This early depiction has the first key elements of the depiction of the Egyptian king and his court. Here, we meet a ruler known as 'Scorpion' because his figure is captioned with the sign of a scorpion. He is shown with a tall crown associated with the south of the country. He undertakes a key function of the Egyptian pharaoh: breaking the soil for cultivation and, by extension, acting as guarantor for a successful harvest. The oversized mace head was a symbolic medium for depicting the actions of the king.

NARMER PALETTE

c. 3100 BCE

Greywacke • Height: 63 cm (24 ¾ in.) • From Hierakonpolis, Egypt

EGYPTIAN MUSEUM, CAIRO, EGYPT

The Narmer palette (front pictured) is the quintessential statement of the Egyptians' mythology of kingship. A clear manifesto of royal power, it is also one with multiple layers of symbolism. The excavator James Quibell must have been astounded when he discovered this well-preserved piece at Hierakonpolis. The 'palette' is in fact a tablet not unlike a stela, but is based on the proportions of a cosmetic palette with the area for crushing pigment delineated between the intertwined necks of two griffins on the reverse. The main scene presents a single royal victory of the southern ruler over a northern adversary,

and Egyptologists interpreted this literally after the palette's discovery. In reality, smaller states are likely to have coalesced more gradually than this image suggests. The palette establishes the key rules for the depiction of the pharaoh using conventions that persisted for millennia. Narmer is shown as much taller than his servants and enemies; he raises his arm, holding aloft a mace to smite his foe. In a striking personification, the bearded enemy is shown as a marsh symbol, subjugated by a falcon. There is no question that Narmer is the victorious falcon, confirming an important identification between the ruler and falcon god Horus.

The reverse of the Narmer palette has a depression that echoes the area used in functional cosmetic palettes for mixing pigment. Here this area is delineated by the intertwined necks of two mythical creatures, perhaps betraying a non-Egyptian influence.

Two dog palette

c. 3100 BCE

*Greywacke • Height: 42.5 cm
(16 ¾ in.) From Hierakonpolis, Egypt*

ASHMOLEAN MUSEUM,
OXFORD, UK

From its very beginnings, Ancient
Egyptian ideology strove for order and
defined itself in contradistinction to the
chaos of outsiders. This evocative image
gives a sense of the Egyptians' anxieties in
the period around the time of unification.
The scene is framed by two jackal-like dogs
and a mass of disordered animals both real and
imaginary. This is one of several oversized ceremonial
palettes that still retain the central depression for
crushing pigment. Ceremonial palettes provided an
impressive surface on which to depict quasi-historical
scenes, rendered permanent as gifts for the gods.

Ivory tag depicting King Den

c. 3000 BCE

Ivory • Height: 4.5 cm (1 ¾ in.), width: 5.3 cm (2 ⅛ in.) • From Abydos, Egypt

BRITISH MUSEUM, LONDON, UK

Inscribed tags of ivory or bone are valuable sources of information about state formation in Egypt. This tag comes from the tomb of King Den at Abydos, and was probably used to label commodities supplied for the king's afterlife. Unlike an earlier king called Narmer, who is shown macing another Egyptian foe on his famous palette (see p.28), Den smites a non-Egyptian enemy. This is one of the first examples of codifying the xenophobia that was to be central to the rhetoric of the pharaonic state. Den raises his mace to smite an enemy captioned as 'easterner' – perhaps a Libyan chieftain or simply a personification of the idea of eastern people.

Gebel el-Arak knife

c. 3200 BCE
Ivory, flint • Length: 25.5 cm (10 in.)
Most likely from Abydos, Egypt
LOUVRE, PARIS, FRANCE

Flint was a material of primary importance
to the Egyptian worldview. In addition to
its practical use as an effective material
for cutting tools, it had considerable ritual
significance and was therefore retained
throughout Egyptian history. It is, however,
most associated with early periods and
some of the finest, most technically
accomplished flint blades derive from the
Predynastic period. This ripple-flaked flint
knife has a finely decorated ivory handle. It
depicts a dense bas-relief scene of the Nile
environment with groups of men apparently
engaged in hand-to-hand combat and in
boats. The scene may have been influenced
by Mesopotamian motifs.

Female figurine

c. 3600 BCE
Terracotta • Height: 29.2 cm (11 ½ in.),
width: 14 cm (5 ½ in.), depth 5.7 cm (2 ¼ in.)
From Ma'mariya, Egypt

BROOKLYN MUSEUM, NEW YORK CITY, USA

To modern eyes, the appearance of this
painted terracotta figurine is strange – with
its beaklike head – and possesses a freedom
most unlike other Egyptian art. Yet the
depiction of the human form in this simple,
abbreviated style is attested in both two and
three dimensions in this period. The female
figurine's pose, with arms raised high above
her head, is paralleled in two-dimensional
depictions on decorated pottery of around
the same period and may be a ritual gesture.
The placement of such a figurine may be
connected with the promotion of fertility.

Narmer baboon

c. 3100 BCE

Travertine • Height: 52 cm (20 ½ in.)
Provenance unknown

EGYPTIAN MUSEUM,
BERLIN, GERMANY

This is one of the earliest examples of the large-scale stone sculpture of an animal form, which was to become a feature of later Egyptian art. It represents a hamadryas baboon, an aggressive species that embodies divine power and primal strength. The deity represented was likely the 'Great White One', so-named for an association with the moon. The recesses for the eyes may have been inlaid in another material – although this is not required for dramatic effect. The simple text scratched on the base identifies King Narmer, and it is likely the piece was created and dedicated in his name.

Faience baboon

c. 3000 BCE

Faience • Height: 8 cm (3 ⅛ in.) • From Hierakonpolis, Egypt
FITZWILLIAM MUSEUM, CAMBRIDGE, UK

The impish charm of baboons obscures their serious religious meaning in ancient Egypt. This example is one of a large group of votive objects, intended as gifts for the gods. It is not known whether these items accumulated in the manner supposed for later votives, or whether the temple staff had a monopoly on the production and sale of faience figurines. One suggestion is that faience was discovered by mixing shavings of copper tools with heated quartz sand. The iconography of the baboon parallels the form of a much larger, monumental example (see opposite).

MacGregor Man

c. 3200 BCE
Black basalt • Height: 39.5 cm (15 ½ in.)
Provenance unknown

ASHMOLEAN MUSEUM, OXFORD, UK

Revd William MacGregor had an impressive
collection of Egyptian antiquities and this is
arguably his most famous piece. It depicts
a man with a long pointed beard and penis
sheath. The identity of the man – god, ruler
or elite individual – is unclear. The high state
of preservation, technical accomplishment
and exceptionality of the piece have raised
doubts over its authenticity. However, parallels
have been identified with other excavated
examples of the human figure and most
believe the piece to be genuinely ancient.

Colossal statue of Min

c. 3300 BCE
Limestone • Height: 1.8 m (5 ⅞ ft)
From Coptos, Egypt
ASHMOLEAN MUSEUM, OXFORD, UK

One of three colossal statues representing a
man grasping his erect penis, this distinctive
stance has led to the figure being identified
as an early form of the fertility god Min.
Originally the statue stood over 4 metres
(13 ft) tall, and was set up within or just
outside a temple. The monument is pitted
with a series of abrasions caused by those
hoping to harness the fertility benefits of
the monument by scraping material from it,
probably centuries or even millennia after
the colossus had toppled from its position.

Figure of a man in a boat

c. 4000 – 3500 BCE

Pottery • Height: 8.8 cm (3 ½ in.), width: 11.3 cm (4 ½ in.), length: 23.5 cm (9 ¼ in.) • From Assyut, Egypt

NATIONAL MUSEUM OF ANTIQUITIES, LEIDEN, NETHERLANDS

This figurine is relatively unusual in the context of Egyptian art as a whole because it depicts an uncommon theme: a corpse that is not mummiform. It is one of a series of representations of boats in the Predynastic period, which highlights the centrality of river transport to the Egyptians and was used to conceptualize a route into the afterlife. The deceased – a bearded man – is shown in a foetal position, the most common pose for the body in contemporary Predynastic and early Dynastic burials. The asymmetrical position of the limbs lends an uncommon expressiveness to the figure.

Disc-shaped mace head

c. 4000 – 3500 BCE

Porphyry • Diameter at bottom: 2.4 cm (1 in.), length: 9.1 cm (3 ⅝ in.) • From Adaima, Egypt

BROOKLYN MUSEUM, NEW YORK CITY, USA

For the journey to and existence in the afterlife, many Egyptians – male and female – were provided with weapons. While the inclusion of a mace head may be an indicator of martial skill and therefore social power, the objects are usually too small to do much serious damage – although even a model carried the magical potential to be used as a weapon in the afterlife. The disc shape was designed to cut into the skull with lethal effect. The placement of such a weapon in so many graves perhaps implies that Predynastic Egyptians anticipated some struggle to reach the world beyond, or the prospect of violence when they arrived.

Hieroglyphic offering vessel

c. 3000 BCE

Greywacke • Height: 3.5 cm (1 ⅜ in.), width: 14.5 cm
(5 ¾ in.), length: 17.6 cm (6 ⅞ in.) • From Egypt

METROPOLITAN MUSEUM OF ART, NEW YORK CITY, USA

Egyptian funerary rituals aimed to prolong the
spiritual aspects of the deceased. This vessel highlights
the Egyptian fondness for punning and the interplay
between words and images. Two interlocking signs
make up this object: two arms represent the *ka* spirit,
holding the looped cross or *ankh*, which represents
life. Together they form the essential relationship
between the living and the dead. The *ka* lives
and requires nourishment in the form of
food and drink. The shape of this vessel
encapsulates both the cause
and effect of ritual:
giving offerings so
that the *ka* can
be sustained.

Pottery mask

c. 3500 BCE
Pottery • Height: 20 cm (7 ⅞ in.), width:
18 cm (7 ⅛ in.) • From Hierakonpolis, Egypt
EGYPTIAN MUSEUM, CAIRO, EGYPT

The best interpretation of this enigmatic
face is that it represents a precursor to the
'mummy masks' from later times in Egypt.
Made of straw-tempered pottery covered in
a red slip, it is one of several broken depictions of
the human face found near a tomb in Hierakonpolis.
The moulded detail creates an unusually expressive face
that is absent from later pharaonic art. It should not be ruled
out that the mask once served a function among the living: later
masks with holes for eyes seem to have been used in performances.

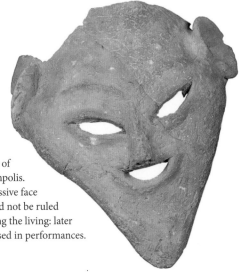

Statue of a seated man

c. 3100 – 2800 BCE

Limestone • Height: 42.5 cm (16 ¾ in.) From Abusir, Egypt
EGYPTIAN MUSEUM, BERLIN, GERMANY

Non-royal individuals joined the ranks of gods and kings in being depicted by statues early in Egyptian history. Stone allowed the eternal participation of a person in offering rituals, even in the event that a corpse was damaged. This early example of a non-royal statue probably came from a tomb chapel and represents the deceased in an archetypally dignified pose: seated on a low seat or stool, with a finely coiffured wig and enveloped in expensive linen garments. This same attitude, with one hand emerging from a cloak, persisted for several millennia. Damage indicates that the eyes were targeted to remove inlays of valuable materials.

The Pyramid Age and After

During the Old Kingdom, a key belief emerged that the pharaoh was the son of the sun god Ra. Full-size boats such as this, found beside Khufu's pyramid at Giza, could have seen functional use during the king's funeral but may also represent a ritual means of transport in the afterlife, where the king could accompany Ra on his celestial journeys.

Between *c.* 2700 and 2200 BCE, Egypt was dominated by the construction of monumental pyramids. This period – termed the Old Kingdom – may rightly be described as the Pyramid Age. These royal tombs clustered around sites to the west of the capital at Memphis, and made serious demands on national resources. Old Kingdom pyramid-building reflects not only an intense belief in the afterlife of the semi-divine king but also a significant practical organization of labour to enable him to achieve it. On present archaeological evidence, temples for the gods do not appear to have been substantial. State resources were focused instead on the king's pyramid project.

The most important development occurred during the reign of King Djoser (*c.* 2667–2648 BCE), at the start of the Third Dynasty. Before this time, kings had been buried in single-storey mastaba tombs built of mud bricks. Imhotep, who served under Djoser in several key roles, appears to have been responsible for the innovative use of stone. By placing one mastaba structure on top of the other, he created a six-stepped pyramid at the site of Saqqara – the

Beginning with the Pyramid of Unas at the end of the Fifth Dynasty, the so-called 'Pyramid Texts' were an essential hieroglyphic guide to the king's afterlife found in later Old Kingdom pyramids. By including these texts, the king was believed to be equipped with knowledge for eternity.

first such stone monument in human history. Importantly, the pyramid did not stand alone in the desert: it was at the heart of an elaborate ritual complex.

Later pyramids were built on the western desert edge, connected to the Nile Valley by a monumental causeway. This architectural link embodies the important connection between living and dead – each required the other for survival. Pyramids were therefore always attached to temples designed to house the perpetual worship of the king's spirit. Stone-built pyramids reached their greatest proportions during the Fourth Dynasty, with the famous monuments of Khufu, Khafre and Menkaure on the Giza plateau.

The king during this period is presented at his most godlike and remote. A new emphasis was placed on the concept of the pharaoh as son of the sun god Ra. While pyramid complexes monopolized most resources, temples to the sun are an exceptional case of Old Kingdom stone temples that survive in recognizable condition.

As a semi-divine intermediary between humanity and the gods, the pharaoh stood at the centre of society. Members of the royal family fulfilled the highest offices of state, with a gradual reduction in this monopoly towards the end of the Old Kingdom. High officials were buried near the king, and these cemeteries were a major arena of monumental display. Non-royal tombs increased in size and complexity as royal pyramids declined in scale, mirroring waning central royal power. From the Fifth Dynasty the interiors of pyramids were covered with extensive inscriptions, the so-called 'Pyramid Texts'. These give the earliest insight into beliefs about the royal afterlife and religious conceptions that were to play a key role in later periods.

From surviving evidence, the pharaoh appears to have been at his most godlike during the Old Kingdom. Here, the face of Pharaoh Menkaure is impassive, with eyes fixed on eternity – an idealized vision of the son of the sun god. Sculptures such as this showed the pharaoh beside, and on a par with, other gods.

The popular image of the Pyramid Age as based on slave labour is a modern fantasy. The workforce, some of whose graves have been excavated, show signs of medical care and attention, and had the honour of being buried near to the pyramid itself. Archaeological remains from settlement sites and recently discovered administrative papyri demonstrate how sophisticated resource management was during the Old Kingdom. Seasonal conscripted work formed part of a national tax system that was well-established at this early point in Egyptian history. The development of long written texts served both administrative and religious purposes.

During the Sixth Dynasty, the power of regional governors increased. The tombs of these officials, such as those located at the southern border (modern Aswan), record expeditions sent out by the king. These accounts provide valuable information regarding Egypt's interactions with neighbouring peoples and indicate an active trade network.

Pepi II, the last king of the Sixth Dynasty, seems to have had a very long reign. This likely contributed to the decentralization of government power, which was also marked by a succession of kings with very short reigns. High officials once closely connected to the capital at Memphis moved away to regional centres. This regionalization resulted in a fragmented state without one overall pharaoh, now known as the First Intermediate period (*c.* 2160–2055 BCE). The monuments of local elites have a distinctive appearance, as they departed markedly from the Memphite court style. More people had the ability to create memorials for themselves, resulting in wider expectations for the afterlife that were once restricted to the highest elite.

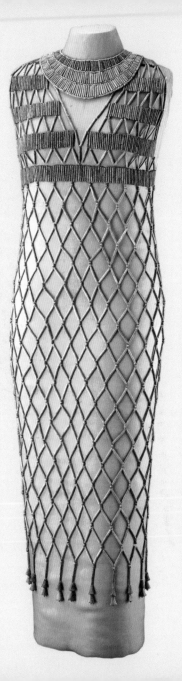

BEADED DRESS

c. 2300 – 2150 BCE
Faience • Length: 1.1 m (3 ¾ ft), width: 73.7 cm (29 in.) • From Giza, Egypt
MUSEUM OF FINE ARTS, BOSTON, USA

As so many objects from ancient Egypt survived having been placed in closed tombs, it is often unclear if objects were used during the life of their owner or made specifically for the tomb. This dress, formed of cylindrical beads and floral pendants, was found by Harvard University archaeologists at Giza in 1933. The beads were restrung only in 2001. One interpretation assumes the dress to have been made exclusively for use of the deceased after death, in part due to the fragility of the arrangement. Yet the same patterns as produced by the beads of this dress appear in paintings and reliefs of dresses in two dimensions, implying that this sort of decoration might have been worn by the living over a linen garment.

An intriguing piece of literature from the Middle Kingdom describes the Fourth Dynasty King Sneferu, who suffers from boredom until he decides to go for a trip on the palace lake. He commanded that he be rowed by young women dressed in fishing nets. Acknowledging the widespread use of wordplay in Egyptian texts, perhaps this faience beadwork was the kind of 'net' being described – and not simply an indication of the monarch's lecherous nature. The diamond-shaped pattern created by the beads continued to appear in depictions of queens and deities, and even persisted into the Roman period on funerary shrouds.

Although undertaking a menial task, Middle Kingdom female 'servant' figures such as this one from Deir el-Bersha appear to wear decorated garments reminiscent of the somewhat earlier beaded dress.

Inlaid chest

c. 2600 – 2400 BCE
Wood with faience and ivory inlays
Height: 19 cm (7 ½ in.), width: 23 cm
(9 in.), length: 38 cm (15 in.) • From
mastaba of Perim, Gebelein, Egypt

EGYPTIAN MUSEUM, TURIN, ITALY

Egyptian art has a special power to appeal to a modern aesthetic. The simple, almost geometric elegance of this piece of furniture resembles a work of art deco design. The two-tone blues of the faience inlays form papyrus stalk shapes, set alongside ivory and wood to striking effect. It should be noted that this remarkably well-preserved piece comes from a regional cemetery and belonged to a non-royal individual. This indicates the level of craftsmanship produced at a distance from the capital, Memphis, for local elites at this time. The small size of the chest may imply it was used to hold jewelry or cosmetics.

Broad collar

c. 2460 – 2320 BCE
*Faience • Length: 27 cm
(10 ⅝ in.), diameter: 19 cm
(7 ½ in.) • From Giza, Egypt*

MUSEUM OF FINE ARTS,
BOSTON, USA

Appreciation of the blues and greens of the semi-precious stones lapis and turquoise made faience (a quartz-based ceramic) extremely popular in jewelry for both men and women. The colour green in particular had connotations of fresh growth and rebirth, and faience jewelry was therefore an appropriate attribute of the deceased in hope of resurrection. This example has been restrung in modern times but the intended arrangement is clear from two-dimensional depictions of such 'broad collars'. While such jewelry could have been worn in life, there is a chance that some pieces were costume jewelry for the dead.

STATUE OF KING DJOSER

c. 2667 – 2648 BCE

Limestone • Height: 1.4 m (4½ ft), width: 45.3 cm (17⅞ in.),
length: 95.5 cm (37⅝ in.) • From the Step Pyramid complex,
Saqqara, Egypt

EGYPTIAN MUSEUM, CAIRO, EGYPT

The Step Pyramid was the world's first major
stone building. Nearby graffiti dating to
this period describe Djoser, the pharaoh for
whom the Step Pyramid was built, as 'the
opener of stone'. This statue depicts Djoser
as seated, wearing the 'heb-sed' jubilee
cloak. There is no evidence that Djoser
lived long enough to celebrate a 'heb-sed'
festival – normally after thirty years' rule.
Yet, through his statue, Djoser's spirit could
magically participate in jubilee rituals
rendered permanently in stone form in the
Step Pyramid complex. The statue comes
from a sealed chamber to the north of the
pyramid, which prevented damage to the
sculpture; an aperture in the wall facing
the statue allowed the spirit of the king
to communicate with the world outside,
even in death. This statue is the earliest
appearance of the striped royal *nemes-*
headdress. Intriguingly, an almost exact
copy of this iconography is known from a
statue some 2,300 years later – suggesting
that Djoser's statue was still accessible in
the Ptolemaic period.

Old Kingdom tomb sculpture was often protected
by a sealed chamber called a 'serdab' (from the
Arabic for 'cellar'). Djoser's serdab is tilted at
13 degrees to enable him to see – and magically
join – the northern stars.

53

Historical calendar

c. 2450 – 2340 BCE
*Basalt • Height: 43.5 cm (17⅛ in.),
width: 25 cm (9⅞ in.)
Provenance unknown*

REGIONAL ARCHAEOLOGICAL
MUSEUM ANTONIO SALINAS,
PALERMO, ITALY

The Egyptian method of writing
history was based on recording
notable annual events, using the
structure of individual kings' reigns.
Sources such as these often took the
form of papyrus copies upon which
monumental inscriptions were based.
This allowed the Egyptians access to
and interest in their own past. This is
the largest piece of several fragments
of a stela recording events from the First
to Fifth Dynasties. Notations of mainly
religious or military events are framed by
curved branches, representing symbols for
'year', with the pharaoh's name and epithets
beneath each section.

Statuette of Khufu

c. 2589 – 2566 BCE
*Ivory • Height: 7.5 cm (3 in.), width: 2.9 cm (1 ⅛ in.),
depth: 2.6 cm (1 in.) • From Temple of Osiris, Abydos, Egypt*
EGYPTIAN MUSEUM, CAIRO, EGYPT

It is ironic that the builder of the largest pyramid in
Egypt is represented in the round only in this tiny
statuette. No other sculpture has survived with
Khufu's name on it. There is, however, the possibility
that this tiny depiction dates from a much later
period, perhaps the Twenty-sixth Dynasty, when
Khufu was a venerated royal ancestor. The king sits
on a throne and wears the red crown of Lower Egypt.
The statuette was headless when first discovered by
W. M. Flinders Petrie's workmen; realizing the
importance of the find, Petrie had them sift
adjacent ground until they located the head.

Statuette of a god

c. 2675 – 2625 BCE
Gneiss • Height: 21.3 cm (8 ⅜ in.),
width: 9.2 cm (3 ⅝ in.) • From Egypt
BROOKLYN MUSEUM,
NEW YORK CITY, USA

The choice of gneiss stone – with its mottled,
partly translucent appearance – evokes
otherworldliness. The identity of this male
figure is, however, uncertain due to the lack
of an inscription or any distinctive iconography.
He is dressed in a belted penis sheath with
full wig, implying that he is a king or more
likely a divinity. This and other early styles
of costume became standard for depictions
of gods throughout pharaonic times, reflecting
their primeval unchanging nature for later
Egyptians. The fine execution of the statuette
suggests that it is the product of a royal
workshop, perhaps destined to be installed
within a king's pyramid temple.

Statues of Rahotep and Nofret

c. 2613–2589 BCE

Limestone • Height of Rahotep: 1.2 m (3 ⅞ ft), height of Nofret: 1.1 m (3 ⅝ ft) From Meidum, Egypt

EGYPTIAN MUSEUM, CAIRO, EGYPT

The remarkable preservation of colour on these statues is thanks in large part to their having been sealed in a closed chamber ('serdab') for over 4,000 years. The serdab was intended to protect statues while making them accessible for rituals. The especially lifelike quality of the statues is heightened by the use of quartz for the eyes. It was said that when the statues were discovered, their glinting gaze startled the excavators. Rahotep was the son of King Sneferu, and (half-) brother of King Khufu, who could commission statues of himself and his wife, Nofret, from the finest artisans.

Offering stand

c. 2500 – 2350 BCE
*Limestone and granite • Height: 42 cm
(16 ½ in.), diameter: 18.5 cm (7 ¼ in.)
From Egypt*

BROOKLYN MUSEUM,
NEW YORK CITY, USA

A key component of the offering
ritual was the burning of incense, an
aromatic mixture of plant gums and
resins. In hieroglyphic script, the word
for incense meant literally 'to make
divine', so the fragrant smoke of the
incense not only created a pleasantly
scented atmosphere for ritual, it also
actively invited and enabled the
presence of both the divine and
the spirit of the deceased to partake
of offerings. This stand is inscribed
for the 'Overseer of the granary,
Irukaptah', and supports a dish
of harder stone. Depictions of
such stands frequently occur
in reliefs but they rarely
survive in the round.

Ewer and basin

c. 2323 – 2150 BCE
*Copper alloy • Height of ewer: 11.5 cm
(4½ in.), diameter of ewer: 11 cm (4⅜ in.),
height of basin: 10 cm (3⅞ in.), diameter
of basin: 20 cm (7⅞ in.) • From tomb of
Tjetji, Saqqara, Egypt*

METROPOLITAN MUSEUM OF ART,
NEW YORK CITY, USA

Purity was an essential requirement of ritual
practice in ancient Egypt. At its most basic,
this involved the pouring of water to cleanse
the body – especially the hands – before rituals.
This metal ewer and basin provided the key
apparatus for ritual performance, both within
temples and in funerary rites. Itemized lists
of such equipment appear in contemporary
papyrus inventories of the contents of temple
goods. The inclusion of this object in a tomb
indicates the importance of purification in
the embalming of the body, the necessity for
purity after death and its relevance as a token
of anticipated offerings for the deceased.

Panel of Hesire

c. 2686 – 2613 BCE
Wood • Height: 1.4 m (4 ⅝ ft)
From Saqqara, Egypt
EGYPTIAN MUSEUM, CAIRO, EGYPT

The use of wood in the decoration of Old Kingdom tomb chapels is hardly attested because it has survived so poorly. Some of the finest carving on wood comes from a long corridor in the tomb chapel of Hesire. Hesire held several priestly titles and one commonly interpreted as 'Chief of Dentists' – a role perhaps allowing him physical access to the king and therefore significant social prestige. Six of at least eleven panels survive, each depicting Hesire with slightly different poses and attributes. These show the tomb owner in a number of different aspects, optimizing the chances that his image would survive for eternity.

Figure of a potter

c. 2450 – 2375 BCE

Limestone and paint • Height: 13.2 cm (5 ¼ in.),
width: 6.7 cm (2 ⅝ in.), depth: 12.5 cm (4 ⅞ in.)
From tomb of Nykauinpu, Giza, Egypt

ORIENTAL INSTITUTE, CHICAGO, USA

The Egyptian elite were obviously concerned about the provision of servants in the afterlife. Unlike an elite gentleman, this sculpture depicts a man in a subservient attitude: crouching at his potter's wheel, apparently naked, in an undignified stance. Pottery making was considered menial, as a later didactic tale advises boys learning to write to avoid being like the potter who is 'muddier with clay than swine'. This man is nameless, in common with the majority of such servant statues, which lack any form of inscription to magically individualize them.

Slab stela

c. 2589 – 2566 BCE
*Limestone and paint • Height: 37.7 cm
(14 ⅞ in.), length: 52.5 cm (20 ⅝ in.),
depth: 8.3 cm (3 ¼ in.) • From
Giza, Egypt*

LOUVRE, PARIS, FRANCE

This finely executed relief represents the most succinct
assurance of perpetual offerings for the deceased. A
range of items are depicted and also carefully listed
above the table in front of Princess Nefertiabet – who
is wearing a leopard-print dress – thus guaranteeing
their eternal availability. Intriguingly, it seems that a
number of these 'slab' stelae were deliberately walled
up and obscured from the sight of the living. Despite
this, they continued to magically function for the
deceased. At later periods, the theme of providing
offerings was expanded to cover the walls of several
rooms. Here it is pared down to a single scene.

Relief of Prince Nefermaat

c. 2613 – 2566 BCE

Limestone and coloured plaster paste
Height: 2.9 m (9 ½ ft), width: 92.7 cm (36 ½ in.),
depth: 8.8 cm (3 ½ in.) • From Meidum, Egypt

ORIENTAL INSTITUTE, CHICAGO, USA

Hieroglyphs were thought to be 'words of the gods'. Originally, the signs themselves seem to have been considered divine. This unique text states that it was made by Prince Nefermaat: 'He made his images [literally "gods"] in writing that cannot be erased'. This must refer to the unusual and labour-intensive technique of executing the decoration in low relief, filled in with coloured paste. Nefermaat's father was King Sneferu, Egypt's greatest pyramid builder in terms of volume. Knowing this, perhaps the prince feared his own name being forgotten. This may have inspired him to commission special decoration as insurance against obsolescence.

False door of Sameri

c. 2450 – 2345 BCE
Limestone • Height: 1.7 m (5 ⅝ ft),
width: 98 cm (38 ⅝ in.) • Most likely
from Saqqara, Egypt

ARCHAEOLOGICAL MUSEUM
OF BOLOGNA, ITALY

The focal point of offerings in Old Kingdom tombs
was an architectural element termed a 'false door'
by Egyptologists. This represented a magical portal
between the sealed subterranean burial compartments
and the open offering chapel for visitors to the tomb.
The 'door' allowed the metaphysical sustenance
provided by offering rituals to reach the deceased
and also enabled – and in some sense channelled – the
deceased in spiritual form to manifest and partake of
offerings. Such offering scenes are frequently depicted,
as in the upper scene here. The fact that the door was
solid prevented physical access to the vulnerable burial
chamber within.

Reserve head

c. 2589 – 2532 BCE
Limestone • Height: 27.1 cm (10 ⅝ in.)
From Giza, Egypt

MUSEUM OF FINE ARTS, BOSTON, USA

Most Egyptian sculpture represents the human
face as generic and stylized. A small group of
about forty limestone heads are, therefore, highly
unusual. These so-called 'reserve heads' mainly
come from elite cemeteries at Giza, and date to the
reigns of the pyramid builders Khufu and Khafre.
Interpretations vary regarding their function. As
they were mostly discovered within tombs, they
may have acted as replacement heads in case of
damage to the body. Deliberate mutilation occurs
on several, perhaps to handicap the potentially
vengeful dead. It is assumed by some scholars
that this head represents an official named
Nefer because it was found in his tomb.

Relief showing harvest rituals

c. 2246 – 2152 BCE

Limestone and traces of paint • Height: 48 cm (18 ⅞ in.), width: 87.5 cm (34 ½ in.) Most likely from Giza, Egypt

BRITISH MUSEUM, LONDON, UK

While the main purpose of tomb chapel decoration was to show the stages in production of offerings for the deceased, sometimes apparently unique incidental details occur. On the top register of this tomb relief are scenes of boat-building; at the bottom harvesting, transporting grain and fishing are illustrated; in the middle register is an unusual depiction of a group of both male and female dancers, flanking what appears to be an individual wearing a mask. To the right, what may be a coming-of-age rite is shown. Once believed to show an exorcism, these activities are probably best interpreted as connected to the harvest.

Tools for 'Opening the Mouth'

c. 2246 – 2152 BCE

Limestone, serpentine, quartz
Palette length: 17.5 cm (6⅞ in.),
width: 9.6 cm (3¾ in.)
From tomb of Impy, Giza, Egypt

MUSEUM OF FINE ARTS,
BOSTON, USA

Images of the gods, the king and the deceased – including the mummified body – needed to be ritually activated in order for the spirit of the deceased to be fully functional in a magical sense. The rite of 'Opening the Mouth' restored or endowed such an image with the powers of sight, speech and movement – the senses enjoyed by the living. In order to effect this activation, a prescribed set of ritual implements were required. These included an implement in the shape of a fish-tailed flint knife and containers for oils and incense. These tools were a model set, roughly carved, acting as tokens of larger pieces used during the funeral.

Tablet for seven sacred oils

c. 2246 – 2152 BCE
Calcite • Height: 7.6 cm (3 in.),
width: 14 cm (5 ½ in.), depth: 1 cm (⅜ in.)
From Abydos, Egypt

BRITISH MUSEUM,
LONDON, UK

The mummification process involved the application of numerous expensive oils, resins and unguents. Oils were also used in offering rituals for the dead and are listed in provisions secured for the deceased. This rectangular tablet provides small dimples for each of seven particularly sacred oils, each labelled with an individual hieroglyphic caption. The phonetic writing of each name is followed by a jar-sign for 'oil'. While acting as an instructive guide for use, the inscription naming the oils was believed to be powerful enough to guarantee that the oils would recur for eternity. The seven sacred oils continue to be mentioned in funerary texts throughout the pharaonic period.

Stele of Nubian soldier Nenu

c. 2124–1981 BCE

Limestone and paint • Height: 37.1 cm (14 ⅝ in.), width: 45 cm (17 ¾ in.), depth: 6.7 cm (2 ⅝ in.) • From el-Rizeiqat, Egypt

MUSEUM OF FINE ARTS, BOSTON, USA

First Intermediate period art is instantly recognizable as it breaks away from prior conventions; when Egypt decentralized, artists in the regions were less constrained by court styles. The resulting artwork may appear naive – especially when, as here, it preserved some of its original bold colour scheme. This is a typical example of funerary art of the period, showing a soldier named Nenu and his wife. His name and distinctive clothing identify Nenu as a Nubian, perhaps a mercenary who fought for an Egyptian faction. The smaller figures are family members, also in Nubian attire, accompanied by hunting hounds.

A Cultural Renaissance

The Middle Kingdom changed the face of the pharaoh. Although still in some sense idealized, the physiognomy of Twelfth-Dynasty kings reflects more of their humanity than earlier rulers. The reaction of the probably small number of people allowed to see statues, such as this one of Amenemhat III, is unknown.

After the decentralization of the First Intermediate period, Egypt's regions coalesced again under King Montuhotep Nebhepetre (*c.* 2055–2004 BCE). This powerful southern ruler established the pre-eminence of his home town, Thebes, and its god Amun, as a focus of royal religious devotion. Montuhotep so began centuries of enlargement of Amun's temple complex at Karnak, and a mutual dependence between the fortunes of the king and the fortunes of Amun.

Royal patronage is reflected in a national programme of embellishing or expanding mud-brick temples and shrines in stone. The mid Twelfth Dynasty saw significant innovations in royal sculpture, with the promulgation of a new facial type. These careworn features are most often associated with Senwosret III and Amenemhat III but continued for several later kings and were taken up by elites. These are unlikely to have been 'portraits' from life; rather, they may carry ideological meanings about the burden of kingship that may be reflected in contemporary texts.

The Middle Kingdom seems to have been an especially 'literary' age. Extensive new works of fiction, later regarded as 'classics', survive as well as informative administrative documents. The ideal of an efficient 'bureaucracy' presented in elite monuments may be misleading. The organizing power of the state can, however, be traced archaeologically in apparently planned settlements, especially in the fortifications along the Nile to the south built to control traffic to and from Nubia, and in the gridlike plans for housing for workers on the king's pyramid project.

Middle Kingdom pyramid complexes remained a colossal expenditure of effort despite the pyramids themselves being largely constructed of mud bricks rather than of solid stone. Associated temples could be vast, as evidenced by the temple next to the pyramid of Amenemhat III at Hawara that became a tourist attraction in its own right during Graeco-Roman times. The finesse of relief carving in Middle Kingdom royal temples is particularly remarkable. This attention to detail and technical skill are echoed in the extremely high quality of surviving (royal) jewelry produced during the Twelfth Dynasty.

Our knowledge of Middle Kingdom high culture is balanced to an extent by the survival of objects from a

Middle Kingdom pyramids tended to be smaller than those of the preceding Old Kingdom, but they were still an important ritual vehicle to launch the pharaoh's spirit into the afterlife. The effort of making millions of bricks for the royal pyramid, such as this of Senwosret II at Lahun, would have provided work for countless people.

The god Amun of Thebes was the patron of the Theban royal line. Here the god presents the hieroglyphic signs for life and endurance to King Senwosret I in his so-called 'White Chapel' at Karnak, thus reciprocating for royal offerings that ensured the proper balance of the cosmos.

non-elite but specialized community of workmen. While not 'non-elite' in the true sense, the workmen of the town of Kahun – servicing the pyramid of King Senwosret II – had unusually high literacy levels and access to resources. Objects from the town bear witness to daily concerns – such as farming, religion, health and play – and are complemented by surviving papyri from the site.

More is known of military activity from the Middle Kingdom than from earlier periods. In biographical texts, participants in campaigns give details of their expeditions in Nubia and the Near East, of the enemies they encountered and of the rewards they received from the king. Other trading contacts with places like the Aegean Islands are illustrated both in imported objects and in motifs found in Egypt, which show a much wider worldview than the Egyptians had previously.

At the same time, the religious landscape of Egypt itself changed physically and metaphorically. At the centre of this change was the god Osiris. Although already mentioned in the Old Kingdom 'Pyramid Texts', Osiris took on a new prominence. His cult centre at the ancient royal cemetery site of Abydos, north of Thebes, became a major site of pilgrimage thanks to the supposed location of his tomb there. Hundreds of statuettes and stelae were left along the processional route used to celebrate the god's resurrection.

Osiris thus acquired greater importance in the funerary realm. Deceased individuals – at least those elites who left some material evidence – hoped to emulate the rebirth of Osiris. This apparent 'democratization' of the rights formerly enjoyed by the pharaoh is attested chiefly by the adaptation of royal 'Pyramid Texts' for inclusion on rectangular 'box' coffins of the elite. These 'Coffin Texts', along with an increased number of surviving tomb goods, are a rich source of information about expectations for the afterlife. Mummy masks developed into sheathlike coverings for the mummified corpse, inner coffins thus took on human ('anthropoid') shapes in imitation of Osiris, the resurrected king. As a result, the deceased in some sense became Osiris by passing into his underworld kingdom, a guarantee of resurrection.

Riqqeh pectoral

c. 1877–1831 BCE
Gold and semi-precious stones • Width: 4.2 cm (1 ⅝ in.)
From Riqqeh, Egypt
MANCHESTER MUSEUM, UK

This chest ornament is less ornate than royal examples of the same period, although it was created using the same *cloisonné* technique. Two wedjat eyes (or 'eyes of Horus') flank a sun disc above two birds on symbols for 'gold'. At the centre is a stylized papyrus umbel suggesting a sceptre – a symbol of power. The pectoral was found still in situ on a mummy. The tomb chamber's ceiling had evidently collapsed, crushing the coffin. Excavators discovered that in addition to the mummy, remains of another body lay nearby – most likely a tomb robber killed by the rockfall while in the act of stealing the jewelry.

Fire-making set

c. 1877 – 1650 BCE

Wood and string • Maximum length: 33.5 cm (13 ¼ in.)
From Kahun, Egypt

MANCHESTER MUSEUM, UK

Fire was a practical necessity. This fire-making set consists of a curved bow drill and fire sticks. Held in place with a stone cap, the string would be wrapped around the sticks to be rotated into dimples in a wooden base. This drilling motion would cause enough friction to produce sparks, which would set fire to kindling such as dried grass. The base shows signs of charring, indicating that this set saw use. Such practical items were also believed to be of use in the afterlife; a similar set was found in King Tutankhamun's tomb.

Basket of tools

c. 1877 – 1650 BCE

Copper, wood and reeds • Height of basket: 19 cm (7 ½ in.), diameter: 14.7 cm (5 ¾ in.) • From Kahun, Egypt

MANCHESTER MUSEUM, UK

The desert conditions of the town of Kahun, built next to a royal pyramid, preserved a unique group of organic and other perishable objects. The contents of this modest basket – so well preserved that it seems only to have been in use yesterday – give a special glimpse into everyday life. This may have been the toolkit of a craftsman working in the village if not on the pyramid itself. Quality timber was a relatively rare commodity and was imported on behalf of the state. Tools such as these could have been used in working timber brought to the royal workers' town.

Gaming board

c. 1814–1805 BCE
Ivory and ebony • Height of board: 6.8 cm
(2 ⅜ in.), average height with pins: 14 cm (5 ½ in.),
width: 10.1 cm (4 in.) • From western Thebes, Egypt
METROPOLITAN MUSEUM OF ART,
NEW YORK CITY, USA

The Egyptians enjoyed a number of different board
games. This complete example from the tomb of
the official Reniseneb has ten playing pieces: five
with jackal heads and five with the heads of hounds.
The aim of the game appears to have been to move
around the board of fifty-eight holes – surrounding
the image of a palm tree – in order to reach a *shen* (or
'protection') symbol at the centre. The *nefer* ('good')
symbol on some positions perhaps conferred extra
benefits. A small drawer under the board could store
pieces or perhaps the knucklebones or dice used to
allow players to advance.

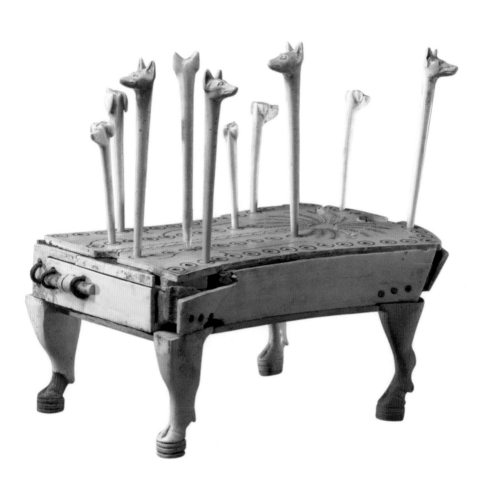

Pectoral and necklace of Princess Sithathoryunet

c. 1887–1813 BCE

Gold, carnelian, lapis lazuli, turquoise, garnet, feldspar • Height of pectoral: 4.5 cm (1 ¾ in.), width of pectoral: 8.2 cm (3 ¼ in.), length of necklace: 82 cm (32 ¼ in.) • From Lahun, Egypt

METROPOLITAN MUSEUM OF ART, NEW YORK CITY, USA

The Middle Kingdom was a high point of technical accomplishment in jewelry making. This is one of the finest examples of royal workmanship. Executed in *cloisonné* on an intricately detailed scale, the pectoral is beautifully inlaid with semi-precious stones. Two falcons – personifications of kingship – grasp symbols for protection. They flank the name of King Senwosret II in a cartouche, which rests on a symbol for 'millions of years' – assuring the king's perpetual majesty and power. The pectoral belonged to Senwosret's daughter and is one of several pieces from a box in her tomb overlooked by tomb robbers.

GIRDLE

c. 1900–1750 BCE

Silver, lapis lazuli, feldspar, electrum, carnelian, amethyst
Length: 47 cm (18 ½ in.), depth: 4.5 cm (1 ¾ in.) • *Most likely from Thebes, Egypt*

BRITISH MUSEUM, LONDON, UK

The Egyptians were concerned to promote fertility – and therefore rebirth – both in everyday life and in the afterlife. This piece of jewelry carries symbols closely associated with femininity, fertility and protection. Women are shown wearing similar items as girdles rather than as necklaces.

Cowrie shells were likened in shape to female genitalia, and some metal examples contained small pellets that rattled softly when the wearer moved, especially when dancing. The fact that these cowrie shapes were soldered from two parts implies the same sound effect was sought here. Such an association between femininity, dance and eroticism was common in pharaonic Egypt. The representations of locks of hair – either sidelocks or, less likely, stylized beards – may evoke the goddess Hathor, who is often shown with her heavy wig bunched in similar elaborate lappets. A lotus flower with a personification of infinity provides a central motif.

One contemporary Middle Kingdom story presents an account of a female troupe rowing the pharaoh's boat on a lake; one girl loses her fish-shaped pendant in the water and a magician has to be summoned to part the waters and retrieve the precious amulet. This attests to the power and significance of items such as those represented on this girdle.

This faience figurine – from a contemporary tomb and now in the British Museum – depicts a woman with truncated legs and wearing a girdle around her waist. Such figurines are often associated with fertility.

Oyster shell with cartouche

c. 1956–1911 BCE

Oyster shell • Height: 10.2 cm (4 in.), width: 10.9 cm (4 ¼ in.) • From Egypt

BURRELL COLLECTION, GLASGOW, SCOTLAND, UK

The name of the pharaoh was magically shielded by being enclosed in a cartouche – an elongated *shen* circle – a powerful symbol of protection. Yet the name of the pharaoh could itself act as an amuletic symbol. This oyster shell is pierced for suspension around the neck and would have afforded the wearer the protection of the king's name. The small number of such inscribed oyster shells – most often with the name of King Senwosret I – have usually been interpreted as military decorations. However, firm evidence for a military connection is lacking and their symbolism is likely to be broader.

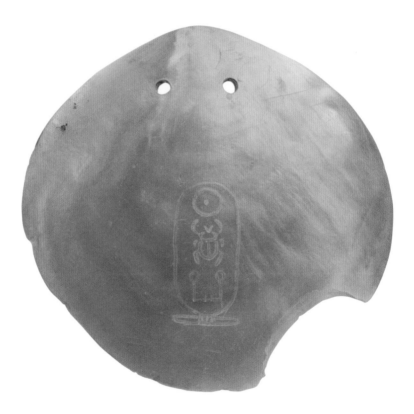

Tale of Horus and Seth

c. 1877–1650 BCE

Papyrus and ink • Height: 14.4 cm (5 ⅝ in.),
width: 39.7 cm (15 ⅝ in.) • From Kahun, Egypt

PETRIE MUSEUM OF EGYPTIAN
ARCHAEOLOGY, LONDON, UK

A large quantity of papyrus scraps were
found among the treasures of everyday life
from Kahun. One of the most entertaining
of these is this fragmentary document.
It carries the earliest version – in cursive,
hieratic text – of a mythological tale
describing the divine adversaries Horus
and Seth. Fighting for the throne of Egypt,
Horus and his uncle Seth engage in a series
of tasks set by other gods to prove one of
them suitable to be king of Egypt. Seth even
attempts to seduce his nephew with the
first-ever recorded 'chat-up line' in history:
'How beautiful are your buttocks!'

Colossal head of Amenemhat III

c. 1831–1786 BCE

*Granodiorite • Height: 83 cm
(32⅜ in.), width: 82 cm
(32¼ in.), depth: 69 cm (27⅛ in.)
From Bubastis, Egypt*

BRITISH MUSEUM,
LONDON, UK

The name and reputation of Amenemhat III as a formidable builder even rivalled those of his successor Ramesses II. Amenemhat constructed a huge temple complex surrounding his pyramid at Hawara in the Faiyum. This incredible structure was visited by Herodotus in the 5th century BCE, who described it as 'The Labyrinth' in his *Histories*. Perhaps because of his vast programme of monumentalization – including statues such as this – Amenemhat III was worshipped as a god even during his own lifetime. This sculpture – moved and reused centuries after the king's death – would have been particularly striking because, unusually for so large a statue, it had separately inlaid eyes of other materials.

Heart scarab of
King Sobekemsaf II

c. 1580–1560 BCE

*Gold and green jasper • Length: 3.8 cm
(1 ½ in.), width: 2.5 cm (1 in.) • From
Thebes, Egypt*

BRITISH MUSEUM, LONDON, UK

Texts in the *Book of the Dead* instruct that an amulet
in the shape of a scarab beetle should be placed on
the chest of the mummified deceased. In order to
reach a blissful afterlife, the Egyptians believed that
a person's heart – the seat of intelligence – had to
be weighed on a set of scales. A 'heart scarab' was
inscribed with a section from the *Book of the Dead*,
instructing the heart not to speak up against the
deceased in the final divine judgment. The looting
of Sobekemsaf's resting place is mentioned in
infamous papyrus accounts of tomb robberies.

Head of Senwosret III

c. 1870–1831 BCE
*Quartzite • Height: 45.1 cm (17 ¾ in.), width: 34.3 cm
(13 ½ in.), depth: 43.2 cm (17 ⅛ in.) • From Egypt*

NELSON-ATKINS MUSEUM OF ART, KANSAS CITY, USA

The face of King Senwosret III is one of the most
immediately recognizable of all Egyptian pharaohs.
This over-life-size sculpture shows the king with his
distinctively hooded eyes, downturned mouth and
large ears. The original intent of the artisans in creating
this remarkably careworn visage is not clear. Perhaps this
represents the king as 'shepherd' of his people, tired with
the burden of rule, concepts expressed in contemporary
literature. As the bodies of Senwosret's statues are always
generically athletic, and his facial features are shared
by non-royals and later kings, it is likely an ideal rather
than a portrait.

Ka statue of Awibre Hor

c. 1700 BCE
*Wood, rock crystal, quartz, plaster, traces of gold
Height: 1.7 m (5 ⅝ ft), width: 27 cm (10 ⅝ in.)
From Dahshur, Egypt*

EGYPTIAN MUSEUM, CAIRO, EGYPT

This striking sculpture was found intact, within a wooden
shrine, laid flat in the king's tomb. It depicts a key aspect
of the spirit of the king: his *ka* (or 'double'), the spirit that
required food and drink offerings after death. Unusually,
the king is shown naked: perhaps a reference to the *ka*
created as a spiritual companion to a human from birth.
The hieroglyphic symbol for *ka* is two raised arms, which
this statue wears on its head. The statue may have been
used for rituals during the king's life and seems to have
been a standard part of later royal funerary goods.

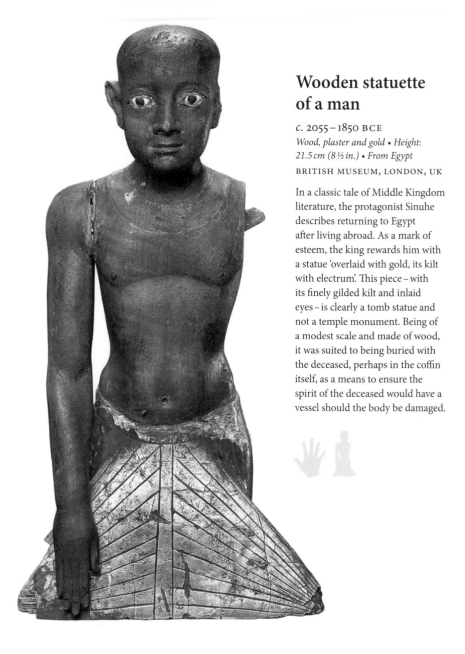

Wooden statuette of a man

c. 2055–1850 BCE
Wood, plaster and gold • Height:
21.5 cm (8 ½ in.) • From Egypt
BRITISH MUSEUM, LONDON, UK

In a classic tale of Middle Kingdom literature, the protagonist Sinuhe describes returning to Egypt after living abroad. As a mark of esteem, the king rewards him with a statue 'overlaid with gold, its kilt with electrum'. This piece – with its finely gilded kilt and inlaid eyes – is clearly a tomb statue and not a temple monument. Being of a modest scale and made of wood, it was suited to being buried with the deceased, perhaps in the coffin itself, as a means to ensure the spirit of the deceased would have a vessel should the body be damaged.

Statue of Sennuwy

c. 1956–1911 BCE
Granodiorite • Height: 1.1 m (3 ¾ ft)
From Kerma, Sudan
MUSEUM OF FINE ARTS, BOSTON, USA

When this and other statues were found by
the American Egyptologist George Reisner
at Kerma, he believed he had uncovered an
Egyptian imperial outpost. In fact, these
statues had been taken by Kerman militias
during raids on tombs at Asyut. Sennuwy
was the wife of the governor of Asyut,
Hepdjefa, whose tomb chapel was carved
with an elaborate contract with priests to
offer to his statues. Ironically, the statues
were stolen a few centuries later. Sennuwy's
statue appears to have been burnt and other
statues were fragmentary, suggesting a
malicious reversal of the execration rituals
the Egyptians practised on the Kermans.

BIRTH TUSK

c. 1875 – 1700 BCE

Hippopotamus ivory • Length: 42 cm (16 ½ in.), width: 5 cm (2 in.)
From Egypt

ANTIKENMUSEUM BASEL, SWITZERLAND

Pregnancy, childbirth and infancy were transitional times that
carried significant danger in ancient Egypt. As much divine help
as possible was enlisted by all members of society, although access
to the type of ritual or magical practice represented by this kind
of object may have been restricted to elites. These objects enabled
mortals to channel and direct the power of the gods – known as
heka in ancient Egyptian – against their supernatural enemies.
Variously referred to as 'tusks', 'knives' or 'wands', these objects
represented a significant weapon in the magical armoury of
the Egyptians against the unknown. The tusks are made of
hippopotamus ivory; female hippopotamuses were well
known to the Egyptians as ferocious, defensive mothers
and were therefore closely associated with women
and children. The images on this piece depict
various deities and demons shown in their most
fearsome aspect – with protruding tongues,
grasping serpents and knives – in an attempt
to ward off evil from mother and child.
Most examples of birth tusks lack any text,
with the purely figural decoration being
sufficient to help achieve magical aims.
Several similar examples show signs of
wear, perhaps having been in contact
with the ground for encircling or
maybe employed more directly in
the delivery of a child.

The leonine god Bes (sometimes referred to as 'Aha', the 'fighter') wards off evil. He is often depicted full-face on birth tusks, grasping serpents. Here he is shown three-dimensionally in such a pose.

Figurine of a
female enemy

c. 1870–1750 BCE
Pottery • Height: 12 cm (4 ¾ in.) • From Egypt
FITZWILLIAM MUSEUM, CAMBRIDGE, UK

Pharaonic Egypt was, in ideological terms, deeply
xenophobic. The Egyptians defined themselves as
separate from – and superior to – all non-Egyptian
peoples. Through the principle of sympathetic magic,
one might harm an individual or entity simply by
naming or depicting them. A series of simple clay
figurines – some with texts listing both physical and
non-physical enemies of Egypt – magically represented
these opponents as subjugated and defenceless. This
figurine represents a naked female enemy, her hands
tied behind her back, with a distinctive Asiatic
hairstyle and indications of tattoos. It was believed that
destroying or damaging the figurine would transfer
negative effects to the enemy groups represented.

Ankh stela

c. 1802–1749 BCE

*Limestone and paint • Height: 51 cm
(20⅛ in.), width: 35 cm (13¾ in.), depth:
5.5 cm (2⅛ in.) • From Abydos, Egypt*

GARSTANG MUSEUM OF
ARCHAEOLOGY, LIVERPOOL, UK

The rise in the cult of Osiris – centred on his reputed
burial place at Abydos – led more people to seek the
promise of eternal life. This stela makes that hope
more explicit than most, as it is designed around
a large *ankh* (life) symbol. The open area in the
loop of the *ankh* cross (above, left) was perhaps
necessitated by a flaw in the stone, and could have
acted as a two-way 'window' in an offering chapel.
The stela is also unusual for the detailed depiction of
agricultural activities on the reverse (above, right),
including a wheeled seed container pulled by oxen.

Medical papyrus

c. 1600 BCE

*Papyrus and ink • Height of page
shown: 33 cm (13 in.), length of
complete scroll: 4.7 m (15 ⅖ ft)
Most likely from Thebes, Egypt*

NEW YORK ACADEMY OF
MEDICINE, NEW YORK CITY, USA

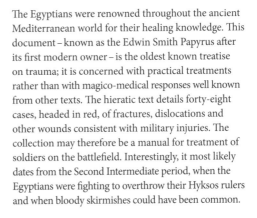

The Egyptians were renowned throughout the ancient
Mediterranean world for their healing knowledge. This
document – known as the Edwin Smith Papyrus after
its first modern owner – is the oldest known treatise
on trauma; it is concerned with practical treatments
rather than with magico-medical responses well known
from other texts. The hieratic text details forty-eight
cases, headed in red, of fractures, dislocations and
other wounds consistent with military injuries. The
collection may therefore be a manual for treatment of
soldiers on the battlefield. Interestingly, it most likely
dates from the Second Intermediate period, when the
Egyptians were fighting to overthrow their Hyksos rulers
and when bloody skirmishes could have been common.

Model boat

c. 2055–1773 BCE
*Mixed media • Length: 71.5 cm
(28 ⅛ in.) • From Beni Hasan, Egypt*
ASHMOLEAN MUSEUM,
OXFORD, UK

Distance transport in ancient Egypt was conducted by
boat. Known chiefly from the Middle Kingdom, the
model boat was an important addition to an elite tomb.
Ideally, the deceased would be provided with two: one
with sail hoisted to catch the northern wind in order
to travel south (as here) and one with oars to enable
the crew to row along with the current to travel north.
The objective of these trips seems to have been to
visit the sacred city of Abydos, last resting place of
Osiris, but model boats allowed the deceased greater
freedom of movement in the afterlife generally.

Soul house

c. 1981–1802 BCE

Pottery • Height: 27.1 cm (10 ⅝ in.), width: 34 cm (13 ⅜ in.), depth: 27 cm (10 ⅝ in.) • From Deir Rifeh, Egypt

MANCHESTER MUSEUM, UK

Most so-called 'soul houses' were found close to the desert surface by the British Egyptologist W. M. Flinders Petrie at the cemetery site of Deir Rifeh in Middle Egypt. Petrie categorized these models into different 'types' based on their architectural features. It is unclear if the models represent houses or tombs, as they show key elements of both. It seems that Petrie's 'soul houses' – for the name has stuck – were associated with the graves of the relatively modest elite. These individuals could not afford to commission the imposing nearby rock-cut tombs, with porticoed facades, of the type the 'soul houses' seem to imitate.

MODEL OF A SLAUGHTERHOUSE

c. 1981–1975 BCE

Wood, plaster and paint • Length: 76.8 cm (30¼ in.), width: 58.5 cm (23 in.) • From Thebes, Egypt

METROPOLITAN MUSEUM OF ART, NEW YORK CITY, USA

This tomb model depicts aspects of food production, which it was hoped would provide spiritual nourishment for the deceased tomb owner for eternity. In the later Old Kingdom, different preparatory stages of farming and animal husbandry had been depicted on tomb chapel walls. In the Middle Kingdom, a more magically efficient means of achieving the same aim was to render activities in three-dimensional wooden models buried in the sealed part of the tomb.

This model shows a functioning area for meat production, giving details that are not otherwise archaeologically attested. Two trussed oxen are shown being dispatched, while butchers catch the blood; elsewhere a goose is plucked, and joints of meat hang out to dry above. Butchery was a high-status, ritualized act, as meat was a prestigious product and was rarely consumed by most of the ancient Egyptian population. This is just one of two dozen such models, of the highest quality, found in a single chamber of the tomb of the Royal Chief Steward Meketre. The tomb owner's close position to the king ensured that he had access to the finest craftsmen.

The slaughter of cattle was an important part of the funeral ritual because the strength of the animal was believed to sustain and enliven the deceased. This contemporary relief scene appears on the sarcophagus of Queen Ashit.

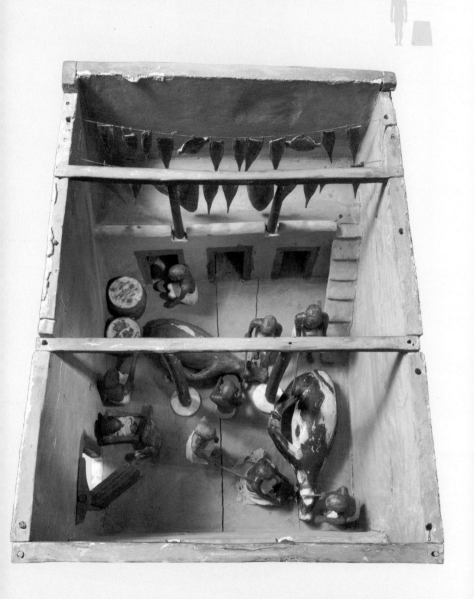

Water vessel

c. 1887 – 1813 BCE
Alabaster • Height: 56 cm (22 in.), diameter:
26.7 cm (10 ½ in.) • From Lahun, Egypt
METROPOLITAN MUSEUM OF ART, NEW YORK
CITY, USA

Egyptians feared many deprivations in the afterlife,
not least going hungry and thirsty. Middle Kingdom
'Coffin Texts' include spells describing how to quench
thirst. This vessel – an impressive stone rendering
of one usually made of faience or metal – carries a
hieroglyphic inscription intended to ensure an eternal
supply of fresh cool water for the deceased princess.
The text makes explicit the function of the vessel's
contents: 'Princess Sithathoryunet, accept these your
cool waters from the earth, which beget everything
living and all things…May you live through them
and be restored through them'.

Box coffin of Seni

c. 1850 BCE

Wood and paint • Height: 73 cm (28 ¾ in.), width: 62 cm
(24 ⅜ in.), length: 2.1 m (6 ⅞ ft) • From Deir el-Bersha, Egypt

BRITISH MUSEUM, LONDON, UK

The Egyptian belief in the magical effectiveness of images
is best illustrated during the Middle Kingdom in coffin
decoration. Rectangular box coffins of this period have two
large painted or inlaid eyes on one side, here painted in a
panel above a depiction of a door. These were located at the
head-end of the coffin, and the body within was laid on its
side to enable the deceased to 'look out' and pass into the
world beyond. The interior of this coffin – belonging to a man
named Seni – is covered with so-called 'Coffin Texts', which
provided a finely illustrated guide to the afterlife.

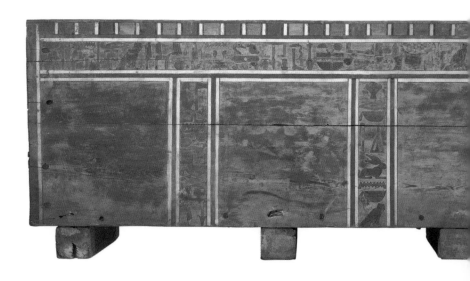

Body coffin of Userhat

c. 1850 BCE

*Wood, plaster and paint • Height 33.2 cm
(13⅛ in.), width: 41.2 cm (16¼ in.), length:
1.8 m (5⅞ ft) • From Beni Hasan, Egypt*

FITZWILLIAM MUSEUM, CAMBRIDGE, UK

In the early Middle Kingdom, coffins for the first
time took the shape of a wrapped human form.
Developing from earlier masks that covered only the
head, the anthropoid coffin provided a carapace for
the entire corpse. It was usually placed within an outer,
rectangular box coffin. Here, Userhat – a soldier – is
shown in radiant white ready for rebirth. The form
of the wig and long beard is an allusion to kingly and
divine regalia, and therefore to Osiris, the one-time
king of Egypt who went on to rule the underworld
after his resurrection. It was this Osirian rebirth
that even non-royal Egyptians hoped to imitate.

Egypt's Golden Age

Gold flowing into Egypt, chiefly from Nubia, funded the rulers of the New Kingdom. An indication of that wealth was contained in the almost intact tomb of Tutankhamun. Jewelry such as this pectoral, of gold and semi-precious stones, provided powerful amuletic protection as well as glitter.

Pharaonic history should not be seen in simplistic terms of 'highs' and 'lows', yet the New Kingdom seems undeniably to have been a period of sustained power and wealth. The strength of the state was forged during the preceding Second Intermediate period when Egypt was ruled by the Hyksos, a people from western Asia. After the Hyksos 'expulsion', the pharaoh led Egyptian forces against Nubia to the south and regions in the Near East. This set profitable relations for Egypt with surrounding territories, although the idea of an Egyptian 'empire' is probably anachronistic.

The Egyptian rulers who led the war against the Hyksos were Theban; royal women played a significant role this time, establishing another theme that would run throughout the New Kingdom. Most sources of written evidence come from Thebes; this may reflect a genuine focus of attention on the home town of the Theban liberators and their patron deity Amun. Yet this impression may be more apparent than real due to the fact so little remains of the once-sprawling city of Memphis in the north (now mostly buried under modern Cairo), and other major centres that have since disappeared.

Ramesses II looms large in the history of ancient Egypt. He had more colossal statues made (or adapted) for him than any other king. The transport of this giant head from his Ramesseum temple to the British Museum in 1816–19 inspired Percy Bysshe Shelley's poem Ozymandias *(c. 1817).*

The outer decoration of major temples focuses on military victories, mainly of the Eighteenth and early Nineteenth Dynasties. Such action is shown as being sanctioned and celebrated by the god Amun. Yet it was not simply that booty from numerous foreign campaigns funded the building of temples in the New Kingdom; rather, the importance placed on building massively in stone at this period reached a scale not seen since the great pyramids of the Old Kingdom. Temple-building favoured certain forms of architecture, notably the obelisk (a solar symbol) and the columned hypostyle hall. Karnak is the best showcase for both.

Through their monuments, the public character of pharaohs of the New Kingdom is much better attested than for their predecessors. The familiarity of Hatshepsut, Tuthmose III, Amenhotep III and Ramesses II is due to their surviving inscriptions and images, but has tended to monopolize attention from other individuals who contributed to the success of New Kingdom Egypt.

Royal self-presentation combined aspects of innovation and archaism. While the pharaoh remained central to Egyptian society, the concept of the king was not as static as is often assumed. The exceptional public personae of the female ruler Hatshepsut and 'heretic' King Akhenaten show how the traditional mantle of kingship could be shaped to suit the incumbent. Ramesses II's was undoubtedly the most wide-ranging monumental celebration of kingship, aided by his having an unusually long, sixty-seven-year reign. Despite his new constructions, Ramesses's masons extensively recycled building materials, departing from the traditional maxim not to 'build from ruins'.

In contrast to temple structures, royal residences seem to have been built of modest materials. Surviving palace sites such as Gurob and Amarna, and the workmen's village of Deir el-Medina, offer insight into New Kingdom domestic settings. While evidence of the high-status industry of glass and faience manufacture survives, relatively little of actual habitations is preserved beyond basic ground plans.

Wealthy burials of the New Kingdom furnish us with the largest number of 'everyday' goods. The resulting impression of a 'take it all with you' attitude is commonly misapplied to all ancient Egyptian tombs. In fact, such objects of daily life may have ritual meanings beyond their practical functions. A marked change is also observable in religious expression generally. The rules of artistic decorum were apparently more subject to change than beliefs themselves. Non-royal people (i.e. those able to commission monuments) were increasingly shown interacting with gods directly. The number of gods, or forms of those gods, proliferated; deified kings such as Amenhotep I were appealed to alongside major gods, such as Amun and Ra, along with more domestic or regionally specific deities.

If taken at face value, this evidence implies a utopian society that believed in a blissful afterlife. Yet, the New Kingdom also provides us with a darker side to the apparent perfection. Laments inscribed in tombs bemoan the state of the dead, and urge people to live for the moment. Papyri recount evidence of socio-economic crisis towards the end of the Twentieth Dynasty, with workers' strikes and brutal punishments for the widespread practice of tomb robbery.

The temples of Karnak created one of the single largest religious complexes in the world. Although inaccessible to the general public, the courtyards and pillared halls would have been busy with temple staff bringing in offerings and maintaining the buildings.

Golden fly amulets

c. 1550 – 1525 BCE

*Gold • Length of chain: 59 cm
(23 ¼ in.), length of flies: 9.3 cm
(3 ⅝ in.), maximum width of flies:
6.8 cm (2 ⅝ in.) • From Thebes, Egypt*

EGYPTIAN MUSEUM,
CAIRO, EGYPT

Flies were one of several insects depicted in Egyptian amuletic jewelry, although the precise symbolism of the fly is uncertain. The Egyptian pantheon lacks, for example, a fly god. Perhaps because of their tenacity and persistence, they may have been associated with military endeavour. An association with the bloody battlefield may also be appropriate for flies. Golden flies have often been interpreted as something akin to a military decoration because of their association with Queen Ahhotep – often viewed as an Amazonian-style queen who, according to one text, mustered troops on her own. This may be a misinterpretation, however, and the amuletic value of flies is probably underestimated.

Cosmetic spoon

c. 1550 – 1250 BCE

*Wood and ivory • Length: 29.3 cm
(11 ½ in.), width: 5.5 cm (2 ⅛ in.)
From Egypt*

LOUVRE, PARIS, FRANCE

The New Kingdom witnessed a particular interest in naturalistic forms. This cosmetic spoon depicts a swimming female, a seemingly playful arrangement that bends the formal conventions of Egyptian art. The girl holds out in front of her a dish in the form of a duck – a common motif in the Eighteenth Dynasty, which implies new life because ducks emerge from the reed thickets at dawn with the rising sun. Underneath the duck's moveable wings, the 'spoon' is shaped as a protective cartouche, and is decorated with tilapia fish – another symbol of rebirth.

STRIATED GLASS VESSEL

c. 1400–1200 BCE
Glass • Height: 6.3 cm (2½ in.), width: 5.4 cm (2⅛ in.) • From Egypt
GETTY MUSEUM, LOS ANGELES, USA

Glassmaking technology first flourished in Egypt about the middle of the Eighteenth Dynasty. Raw materials and evidence of the glassmaking industry are attested from Egyptian elite centres such as palaces. Items made of glass were the height of luxury, and this piece is likely to have held considerable value. Its small size indicates that it once contained prized perfumed oil.

As in other ancient Near Eastern forms of glassmaking, most Egyptian glass vessel shapes were inspired by forms that already existed in materials like clay or stone. However, this lentoid or lentil-shaped form may have developed in glass alone and influenced other media rather than the other way around. To create this vessel, the glassmaker heated coloured glass rods and gathered them around a core – made of organic material such as animal dung or clay – supported by a rod. After the shape was formed, the handles and feathered pattern were added by dragging an implement across the coloured, molten glass. Once the finished vessel had slowly cooled, the core was removed from inside.

New Kingdom Egypt was a hub for international trade in the eastern Mediterranean. Wealthy officials included cosmopolitan scenes of non-Egyptian 'tribute' bearers bringing goods to Egypt in their tomb chapels, as in this example from the Theban tomb of Sobekhotep.

Pair of sandals

c. 1390 – 1352 BCE

Grass, reed and papyrus • Left foot: Height: 11 cm (4 ⅜ in.), width: 9 cm (3 ½ in.), length: 30.4 cm (12 in.); Right foot: Height: 8.8 cm (3 ½ in.), width: 10.5 cm (4 ⅛ in.), length: 30.4 cm (12 in.) • From the Valley of the Kings, Thebes, Egypt

METROPOLITAN MUSEUM OF ART, NEW YORK CITY, USA

Elite Egyptians wore a wide variety of footwear, from the most basic sandals to richly decorated shoes. This simple pair of sandals is made of plaited grass and reeds, with the toe and side straps made of split papyrus. They could have been worn in life but, by being included in a tomb, were expected to be of use in the afterlife. The pair comes from the almost intact tomb of a wealthy couple named Yuya and Tjuyu, the parents-in-law of King Amenhotep III. Footwear also implies freedom of movement, something the Egyptians wanted to enjoy for eternity.

Merit's cosmetic box

c. 1390 – 1352 BCE

Wood, paint, faience, glass and alabaster
Height: 22 cm (8 ⅝ in.), width: 29.5 cm
(11 ⅝ in.), length: 49 cm (19 ¼ in.)
From Deir el-Medina, Egypt

EGYPTIAN MUSEUM, TURIN, ITALY

The Egyptians cared about their appearance. This selection of cosmetic containers is from the intact tomb of the 'Overseer of Works' in the Valley of the Kings, Kha, and his wife, Merit. Both men and women wore make-up and jewelry, although hieroglyphs label the box as belonging to Merit. Vessels are made from a range of expensive materials – glass, faience and alabaster – although the box containing them is somewhat crudely decorated. Being in charge of works at the Valley of the Kings, Kha could acquire luxury items and commission a range of services from workmen under his charge.

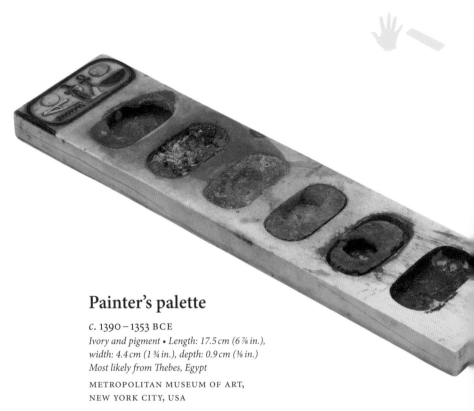

Painter's palette

c. 1390 – 1353 BCE
Ivory and pigment • Length: 17.5 cm (6 ⅞ in.),
width: 4.4 cm (1 ¾ in.), depth: 0.9 cm (⅜ in.)
Most likely from Thebes, Egypt

METROPOLITAN MUSEUM OF ART,
NEW YORK CITY, USA

While a scribe's palette usually has only two wells
for black and red paint, this palette holds six colours.
Paint applied for wall decoration is likely to have been
mixed on a larger plate or vessel. It is therefore likely
that this more delicate ivory palette was used in the
production of a manuscript with coloured illustrations,
such as the *Book of the Dead.* The cartouche gives the
name of King Amenhotep III, under whose reign a
number of brightly coloured *Book of the Dead* papyri
were produced. A reed pen or narrow brush would
have been used with water to mix the pigment.

Stirrup jar

c. 1390 – 1250 BCE

*Faience • Height: 10.5 cm
(4 ⅛ in.), width: 12 cm (4 ¾ in.)
From Gurob, Egypt*

MANCHESTER MUSEUM, UK

The palace complex at Gurob was a diverse, international community as the home to several non-Egyptian women who had been given to the pharaoh as wives to seal diplomatic ties. Arriving in Egypt with retinues of servants, these women brought a range of imports from the ancient Near East. Egyptian artisans copied non-Egyptian forms – like the Canaanite stirrup jar – in Egyptian faience and added their own decoration. The elegant black outlines of this vessel reference the natural world, taking the shape of pendant lotus flowers, ducks and the symbol for water. These are especially common motifs in palaces of the mid to late Eighteenth Dynasty.

Kohl tube

c. 1360 – 1352 BCE
Faience • Height: 14.4 cm (5 ⅝ in.), diameter:
1.8 cm (⅞ in.) • From Egypt
METROPOLITAN MUSEUM OF ART, NEW
YORK CITY, USA

Egyptians of both sexes wore eye make-
up – for aesthetic effect and to counter the
glare of the sun. This tube is designed to hold
kohl, and is shaped for use with a long thin
applicator. It carries a hieroglyphic text that
allows us to date the piece quite precisely,
because it names King Amenhotep III and
his daughter Sitamun, who became his queen
about his thirtieth year on the throne. This
role was probably a ritual one, in connection
with the 'heb-sed' jubilee the king celebrated
after thirty years, placing the manufacture of
this piece in the last years of his reign.

Servant girl statuette

c. 1390 – 1352 BCE
*Wood and traces of gold • Height: 14.9 cm (5⅞ in.),
width: 3.6 cm (1⅛ in.), depth: 8 cm (3⅛ in.)
From Egypt*

ORIENTAL MUSEUM, DURHAM, UK

This carrying girl is shown naked save for a
girdle around her waist and a necklace with
an amulet of the god Bes. The contrapposto
appearance of the figure makes it seem
quite unlike the rigid frontality of most
Egyptian sculpture. The container she holds
was for eye-makeup, allowing a degree of
sensuousness and informality that would not
be permitted in a stone statue. While she may
have been considered delightful for the living
beholder, the figurine's sexuality would also
promote the rebirth of the deceased when
placed in a tomb context.

Window grille

c. 1213 – 1203 BCE

Limestone • Height: 1.2 m (3 ⅞ ft), width:
79 cm (31 ⅛ in.) • From Memphis, Egypt

PENN MUSEUM, PHILADELPHIA, USA

Most ancient Egyptian palaces, like the
dwellings of ordinary mortals, were made
of mud brick and have not survived the
ravages of time. The palace of Merenptah
at Memphis, however, had many elements
made of stone. It is unclear therefore if
this building was intended for use as a
real residence or as a ritual space as part
of a nearby temple complex. The grille is
decorated with *djed* 'stability' symbols,
papyrus plants and crouching sphinxes –
each appropriate to the decoration of
a palace – and would have served as a
clerestory window high up on a wall.

Ostracon with a sketch

c. 1295 – 1150 BCE

Limestone and paint • Length: 15.5 cm
(6 ⅛ in.), width: 14 cm (5 ½ in.) • Most likely
from Deir el-Medina, Egypt

FITZWILLIAM MUSEUM,
CAMBRIDGE, UK

Many rough flakes of limestone – called
ostraca – survive from the workers' village
of Deir el-Medina. Most bear rough
texts, and those with images often have
religious themes. This sketch, however,
leaves a modern audience in little doubt
that it is a caricature, likely of one of
the workmen in the village, possibly
a stonemason. The man is bald and
unshaven, and is shown – unusually
for Egyptian art – with his mouth open.
He is shown actively at work, using a
mallet and a chisel.

Belt of Ramesses III

c. 1182 BCE

*Linen • Length: 5.2 m (17 ft), width:
12.7–4.8 cm (5–1 ⅞ in.) • From Egypt*

WORLD MUSEUM, LIVERPOOL, UK

One of the rarest items to survive from royal tombs is clothing, because it is so fragile. Even in the exceptional setting of Tutankhamun's almost intact tomb, his wardrobe was not well preserved. It is all the more astounding therefore that this belt or girdle of Ramesses III was found intact. It likely originated in the king's tomb. A 'Year 2' date and the royal name were inked on the dangling 'apron' of the belt but were destroyed by a conservation technique. The belt is estimated to have taken three to four months to complete.

Palace tiles

c. 1184 – 1153 BCE

*Polychrome faience • Height: 26 cm
(10 ¼ in.), width: 6.5 cm (2 ½ in.)
From Medinet Habu, western
Thebes, Egypt*

MUSEUM OF FINE ARTS,
BOSTON, USA

The interiors of palaces – even
as small and ritualized as the one
at Medinet Habu in Thebes – were
richly decorated, especially those
that were accessible to visiting
dignitaries from Egypt and
abroad. These tiles depict various
subjugated enemies of Egypt:
here, Nubians with distinctive
hairstyles and clothing. Other
tiles are known showing Asiatics
and Libyans. These Nubians are
shown with their hands tied and
would likely have decorated a
surface on which the king would
have walked, magically crushing
his enemies underfoot. The
colourful, lustrous appearance
of these glazed tiles would
have created a striking – and
intimidating – impression
for palace visitors.

Kamose stela

c. 1550 BCE
Limestone • Height: 2.3 m (7 ½ ft),
width: 1.1 m (3 ⅝ ft), depth:
28.5 cm (11 ¼ in.) • From
Karnak Temple, Egypt

LUXOR MUSEUM, EGYPT

After around a century of Hyksos
rule, the Egyptians fought to
overthrow their foreign masters. A
key player in the 'war of liberation'
was Kamose. His successor, and
probable brother, Ahmose went on
to establish the Eighteenth Dynasty
and with it Egypt's 'Golden Age'.
The text of the stela uses vivid
language to describe the political
situation. This was one of at least
two stelae set up by Kamose, or
by a successor, to commemorate
his victories. This, the 'second'
stela, describes the capture of a
Hyksos messenger – and enemy
intelligence – by Egyptian forces.

Statue of Hatshepsut

c. 1473–1458 BCE

*Crystalline limestone and paint • Height: 1.9 m (6 ¼ ft),
width: 49 cm (19 ¼ in.), depth: 1.1 m (3 ⅝ ft) • From Deir
el-Bahri, Thebes, Egypt*

METROPOLITAN MUSEUM OF ART,
NEW YORK CITY, USA

Queen Hatshepsut was the most successful of several
female rulers in ancient Egypt. The daughter of
one king, the widow of another and stepmother
of a third, she gradually transformed her image
from queen to male pharaoh. This statue shows
the process in its transitional stage, when
Hatshepsut is still recognizable as a
woman – with indications of breasts –
yet she also wears the traditionally male
nemes-headdress, short kilt and bull's
tail of the pharaoh. The hieroglyphic
inscription on the statue identified
her with kingly epithets, but with
feminine grammar.

Statue of Senenmut and Princess Neferure

c. 1473 BCE
Granodiorite • Height: 72.5 cm (28 ½ in.), width: 24 cm (9 ½ in.) • From Karnak Temple, Egypt
BRITISH MUSEUM, LONDON, UK

Elite temple sculptures were designed to attract the attention of passers-by. This statue depicts Senenmut, a leading official under Queen Hatshepsut and tutor to her daughter Neferure. This piece dates early in Hatshepsut's reign before she had the title 'pharaoh'. The princess is shown enveloped in Senenmut's cloak in an unusual gesture of intimacy that may have shocked contemporary observers. Senenmut invented several new types of sculpture, and it is typical of him to vaunt such closeness to the royal family. It has even been suggested that Senenmut was Neferure's father.

Sphinx of Hatshepsut

c. 1473 – 1458 BCE
*Granite and paint • Height: 1.3 m
(4 ¼ ft), length: 2.8 m (9 ⅛ ft)
From Deir el-Bahri, Thebes, Egypt*

EGYPTIAN MUSEUM,
BERLIN, GERMANY

The sphinx was the most powerful and awe-inspiring form that the pharaoh could assume. Little wonder, then, that it was chosen by the female pharaoh Hatshepsut to demonstrate her strength and legitimacy as ruler. Unlike the normally female sphinx of Greek mythology, the Egyptian sphinx form allowed for gender ambiguity and therefore was suited to Hatshepsut's presentation for her kingship. Some twenty years after her death, for reasons of dynastic succession, Hatshepsut's image was actively persecuted. This sphinx is reconstructed from many different fragments, and was one of the queen's many sculptures from her mortuary temple smashed in ancient times.

Libation vessel

c. 1479–1425 BCE

Silver • Height: 19.5 cm (7 ⅝ in.),
diameter: 13 cm (5 ⅛ in.)
From Thebes, Egypt

METROPOLITAN MUSEUM OF ART,
NEW YORK CITY, USA

Egyptian kings of the New Kingdom cemented
alliances with foreign powers through marriage.
This elegant vessel comes from the tomb of one of
the wives of Tuthmose III. The lady had the rather
un-Egyptian name of Menwi – spelt phonetically in
hieroglyphs – and probably came to Egypt from the
Near East. Etched with an inscription stating that they
were given as 'gifts' from the king, such vessels are
an indication of the richness of the palace – enriched
further by Tuthmose III's extensive campaigns abroad –
perhaps not far from where his foreign wives grew up.

Glass ingot

c. 1352–1336 BCE

Glass • Height: 14 cm (5 ½ in.), width:
8 cm (3 ⅛ in.) • From Amarna, Egypt

GARSTANG MUSEUM OF
ARCHAEOLOGY, LIVERPOOL, UK

Glassmaking was a prestigious industry in the ancient
Near East and glass products were prized around
the Mediterranean for their bright colours. Glass
workshops have been discovered at several Egyptian
palace sites – notably at Akhenaten's capital of Amarna.
The raw materials for glass, such as this ingot, may
have been imported or traded, reflecting the reach and
interconnectedness of international commerce of the
time. Similar glass ingots were found on the Uluburun
shipwreck, which sank off the coast of modern Turkey
around the end of the Amarna period.

STATUE OF AKHENATEN

c. 1352–1336 BCE

Sandstone • Height: 1.3 m (4¼ ft), width: 88 cm (34⅝ in.), depth: 60 cm (23⅝ in.) • From Karnak, Egypt

LOUVRE, PARIS, FRANCE

Once described as 'the first individual in History', King Amenhotep IV – who later changed his name to Akhenaten ('servant of Aten') – made the most striking departure from traditional presentations of Egyptian kingship. Here, the king appears at his most extreme. He has his hands crossed, holding the traditional sceptres of royal power: the crook and flail. The chunky name stamps that protrude from the chest and wrists carry the names of the god Aten, in cartouches. Their unusual position has been interpreted by some scholars as an indication that the colossi originally belonged to Amenhotep III, and were recut by his son.

The most distinctive Amarna features are exaggerated here: a long, thin face; narrowed, slanting eyes; full lips and pronounced breasts. These have often been interpreted as signs of sensuousness, decadence and moral turpitude. It is, however, worth considering their original context in a temple structure at Karnak, where the colossi would have appeared less attenuated when viewed from ground level. The statues were deliberately dismantled and buried after Akhenaten's reign, in an attempt to obliterate his memory – though, ironically, this has preserved the distinctive features of Akhenaten in good condition.

Akhenaten's buildings at Karnak were made up of small blocks of stone to enable their rapid construction. They depict a new style of representing the king, engaged in rituals for his favoured god, Aten.

Cuneiform tablet

c. 1390 – 1352 BCE

Pottery • Height: 30.7 cm
(12 ⅛ in.), width: 17.2 m
(6 ¾ in.), depth: 4.5 cm (1 ¾ in.)
From Amarna, Egypt

MUSEUM OF THE ANCIENT
NEAR EAST, BERLIN, GERMANY

Cuneiform script has a distinctive appearance due
to being written with a wedge-shaped stylus. It was
used to record the Akkadian language – the written
lingua franca of diplomatic exchanges in the fourteenth
century BCE. A chance discovery in the ruins of the
royal palace at Amarna led to the unearthing of an
archive of cuneiform tablets, with about 400 examples
now known. Many date to before Akhenaten's reign,
implying they were deliberately retained. Most of these
are letters between kings. Some, like this one, were sent
by the king of Mitanni (northern Syria), Tushratta, and
are addressed to King Amenhotep III. Tushratta opens
by addressing 'my brother' with good wishes for him,
his family and his people. The tone of the letters is at
once eager to please the pharaoh, often listing presents
sent, but some make direct requests and demands for
gifts in return. Unfortunately, the Egyptian side of the
discussion is not preserved.

Statue of Queen Tuya

c. 1390 – 1213 BCE

*Granite • Height: 2.2 m (7 ¼ ft), width: 56 cm
(29 ⅞ in.), depth: 85 cm (33 ½ in.) • From the
Ramesseum, Thebes, Egypt*

VATICAN MUSEUMS, ROME, ITALY

After the pharaoh himself, his principal wife was
the most frequently represented subject in over-
life-size sculpture. This impressive statue of a queen
was originally carved as a monument of Queen
Tiye, the wife of Amenhotep III. A century or so
later, the statue was recarved as an image of Queen
Tuya by her son Ramesses II – a notorious usurper
of monuments – for his own mortuary temple,
the Ramesseum. The statue caught the attention
of Emperor Caligula, who had the partially broken
sculpture transported to Rome. Once installed,
the statue was restored with misinterpreted
iconography on its back pillar.

Anubis shrine

c. 1336 – 1327 BCE
Wood, gold and paint • Height: 1.1 m (3 ⅝ ft),
width: 52 cm (20 ½ in.), length: 2.7 m (8 ⅞ ft)
From the Valley of the Kings, Thebes, Egypt

EGYPTIAN MUSEUM, CAIRO, EGYPT

The almost-intact tomb of Tutankhamun yielded
the most complete 'set' of objects from any New
Kingdom royal burial. The jackal god Anubis was
guardian of the necropolis and master of the ritual
of mummification. Within the shrine on which
his statue rests several objects connected with
mummification were found. The shrine was provided
with two poles to carry it in procession. Like most of
the statues in the tomb, the Anubis figure had been
shrouded in linen; this carried an ink inscription
dated to the seventh year of Akhenaten. Fragments
of similar jackal statues indicate their presence in
other royal tombs.

BUST OF NEFERTITI

c. 1352–1336 BCE

Limestone, plaster and paint • Height: 48 cm (18 ⅞ in.)
From Amarna, Egypt

EGYPTIAN MUSEUM, BERLIN, GERMANY

Perhaps the most iconic image of a woman from the ancient
world, the bust of Nefertiti is difficult to contextualize because
it seems so exceptional. That the uninscribed head is indeed
Nefertiti and not another Amarna royal woman is indicated
by her tall, flat-topped blue crown with colourful ribbon.
The bust is likely to have had a functional role as a model on
which to base others in an artisans' workshop. Plentiful other
archaeological evidence was found for trial pieces from a
sculptors' 'studio' – including a badly damaged companion piece
depicting Akhenaten. The aesthetic appeal of the face should
not seduce us into believing that this is what Nefertiti actually
looked like. Amarna art is full of distortions and stylizations,
despite often being praised for its naturalism. The uniqueness
of the bust has led to (apparently ill-founded) suggestions
that it is a fake; the circumstances of the excavation in 1912
that brought her to light have placed Nefertiti at the centre
of the debate on repatriation of Egyptian antiquities.

*The ancient name of the city
of Amarna was Akhet-Aten
('Horizon of the Aten'). It
was abandoned shortly
after the end of Akhenaten's
reign, leaving many features
of urban life – including
artisans' production
areas – well preserved.*

Sketch of a pharaoh

c. 1294–1143 BCE
*Limestone and paint • Height: 18.5 cm (7¼ in.),
width: 14.6 cm (5¾ in.), depth: 2.9 cm (1⅛ in.)
From Thebes, Egypt*

WALTERS ART MUSEUM,
BALTIMORE, USA

Informal images of the pharaoh are rare.
Flakes of limestone (ostraca) were used
by artisans to plan larger formal scenes
for tomb and temple walls, but also for
informal sketches. This drawing may have
been a trial piece for a monument, as it
also carries drawings of hands. Unusually,
it shows the pharaoh with naturalistic beard
growth, which elsewhere is associated with
mourning. The king wears the blue crown
associated with coronation rites; perhaps
therefore this is a sketch of a new king in
a period of mourning for his predecessor.

Conspiracy papyrus

c. 1153 BCE
*Papyrus and ink • Height of page
shown: 41 cm (16⅛ in.), length of
complete scroll: 5.4 m (17¾ ft)
From Thebes, Egypt*

EGYPTIAN MUSEUM,
TURIN, ITALY

The murder of a pharaoh was an unspeakable crime.
A glimpse into the clandestine world of harem
conspiracies is provided by this unique document
describing court proceedings. The suspects are a
group of men and women charged with plotting the
assassination of Ramesses III to advance the claims
of a certain heir to the throne. It was uncertain if
the plot had in fact succeeded. Apparently conclusive
evidence was provided by a recent CT (computed
tomography) re-examination of the mummy of
Ramesses III, which indicated that he died from major
trauma to his throat. The papyrus records that the
guilty parties were permitted to take their own lives.

ACCOUNT OF A TOMB ROBBERY

c. 1118 BCE

*Papyrus and ink • Height: 25.6 cm (10 in.), length:
40.4 cm, (15 ⅞ in.) • From Thebes, Egypt*

WORLD MUSEUM, LIVERPOOL, UK

The Egyptian ideal of a blissful eternity for the dead is
seriously undermined by the widespread evidence of
tomb robbery, apparently often perpetrated quite soon
after the burial. The New Kingdom royal cemetery
in the Valley of the Kings was particularly prone to
criminal activity due to the richness of its contents.
The security of these hidden burials was compromised
by the knowledge of those living and working near the
royal tombs. By the end of the New Kingdom, western
Thebes had suffered from workers' strikes due to
unpaid wages and violent raids from desert-dwelling
Libyan nomads. Such desperate times resulted in a rise
in thefts, as local people exploited a reduction in, or
absence of, necropolis security.

While tomb robbery in the Valley of the Kings is
known from earlier, during the Eighteenth Dynasty,
an uncompromisingly bright light is shone on thefts
during the last years of the New Kingdom. This
papyrus is one of several documents transcribing
court proceedings concerning individuals accused
of criminal activity. These accounts describe the
examination under torture of some influential
officials – including royal butlers. These men were
eventually found guilty of stealing from the royal
tombs. The punishment, unsurprisingly, was death.

The Valley of the Kings is set in a quiet, relatively remote desert valley. This enabled necropolis officials to control access to the restricted royal burial ground and maintain security throughout most of the New Kingdom.

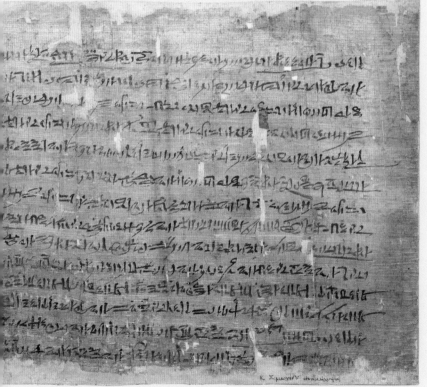

Plan of a royal tomb

c. 1153 – 1147 BCE
*Papyrus and ink • Height: 35 cm
(13 ¾ in.), length: 1.2 m (3 ⅞ ft)
From Thebes, Egypt*

EGYPTIAN MUSEUM, TURIN, ITALY

Blueprints of ancient Egyptian buildings are usually confined to works of fiction. This papyrus plan is unusually informative as it gives the Egyptians' own designations for parts of a royal tomb: the burial chamber is the 'gold house'; there is a 'chariot hall' and a 'shabti place' – both names for rooms related to their contents. The plan accords closely with the layout of the tomb of Ramesses IV. It may not be an architect's sketch but rather a record of the dimensions of the tomb once complete. Necropolis officials may have had to keep records of the size and location of tombs to prevent accidental collision when building new tombs and to monitor security.

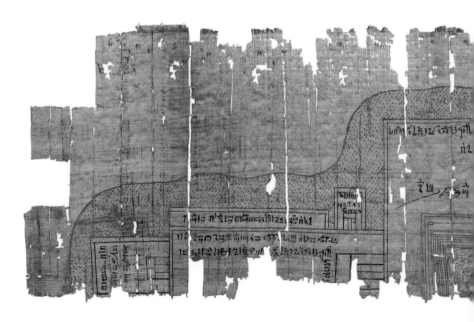

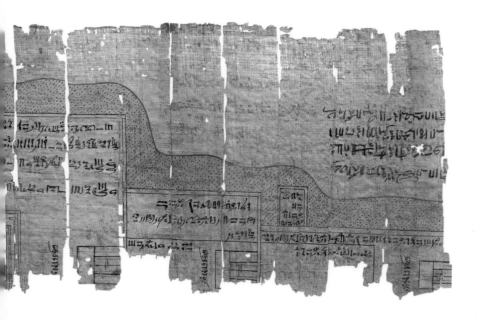

Magical sceptre

c. 1427–1400 BCE

*Faience • Height: 2.2 m (7 ft), width: 25 cm
(9 ⅞ in.), depth: 48.2 cm (19 in.) • From
Naqada, Egypt*

VICTORIA AND ALBERT MUSEUM,
LONDON, UK

This is perhaps the largest single object made
from faience, a glazed ceramic. It takes the
form of a *was*-sceptre, a symbol of power
and dominion. The top of the sceptre is
shaped like an animal head, although it is
uncertain exactly which animal is intended.
Some scholars have suggested a donkey or
the mythical animal associated with Seth,
the god of chaos. Given that this ritual object
was found within a temple of Seth, this may
be an intended association. The sceptre was
deliberately buried in a so-called 'foundation
deposit' in the reign of Amenhotep II to ensure
the eternal stability of the temple.

Stick shabti

c. 1500 BCE
Wood • Length: 13.5 cm (5 ⅜ in.)
From Aswan, Egypt
MANCHESTER MUSEUM, UK

The crude appearance of these objects has led to them being termed 'stick' or 'peg' shabtis. Unlike most shabtis, however, these figurines were not sealed within the tomb to magically undertake tasks for the deceased in the afterlife. Instead they have usually been discovered in the courtyards of early Eighteenth Dynasty tombs, and seem to have been left in the outer parts of tombs as offerings or perhaps tokens of a visit. Rather than the usual 'shabti spell' they carry basic offering prayers, naming the deceased or the donor.

Mummified pigeon

c. 1525 – 1504 BCE
Linen, wood, resin and animal remains • Length of box: 35.5 cm (14 in.) • From Deir el-Bahri, Thebes, Egypt

MUSEUM OF FINE ARTS, BOSTON, USA

It was widely believed that the spirit of the deceased would require sustenance in the form of food and drink after death. Ideally, this would be provided by family members in person, or by images or models in tombs. Occasionally, however, real meals were provided in the form of cooked meat – such as joints of beef or duck – covered in resin to help preserve them: a mummified menu for the dead. These so-called 'victual mummies' are only rarely attested and were apparently confined to New Kingdom Theban tombs.

Scribe statue of Amenhotep, son of Hapu

c. 1390 – 1352 BCE

Granodiorite • Height: 1.3 m (4 ¼ ft) • From Karnak, Egypt

LUXOR MUSEUM, EGYPT

Very rarely were deceased mortals promoted to join the ranks of the gods. Amenhotep, son of Hapu, was one such individual. He is shown here in the prestigious pose of a literate man, slightly flabby to indicate wealth, his head tilted downwards as he reads from or writes on a papyrus scroll on his lap. Amenhotep's posthumous veneration was based on his exceptional service under his namesake, King Amenhotep III. He held many titles, including 'Overseer of Royal Works', and was responsible for many ambitious royal constructions. He even had his own temple – an unprecedented honour for a man of non-royal birth.

Stela of Hatiay

c. 1323 – 1295 BCE

*Limestone • Height: 1 m (3¼ ft),
width: 67 cm (26¼ in.) • From
Abydos, Egypt*

NATIONAL MUSEUM OF
ANTIQUITIES, LEIDEN,
NETHERLANDS

King Akhenaten is well known as a revolutionary who swept away most of Egypt's pantheon in favour of his preferred sun god, Aten. The task of restoring traditional religious practice after Akhenaten's demise was a complex undertaking. A man named Hatiay is known to have lived and worked at Amarna as an artisan, where he produced works in Akhenaten's new style. Later, however, Hatiay seems to have switched sides and returned to orthodoxy. He boasts in this funerary inscription about having been initiated into secret knowledge of the old gods and how he remade statues of them.

Relief depicting men dragging statues

c. 1336 – 1323 BCE

*Limestone • Total scene: Height: 59 cm (23¼ in),
length: 2.5 m (8 ft) • From Saqqara, Egypt*

EGYPTIAN MUSEUM, BERLIN, GERMANY

Wall reliefs from Saqqara tomb chapels are of a distinctive, post-Amarna period style and tend to show details of ritual practice that do not appear elsewhere. This relief from the tomb of Maya depicts part of a funeral procession but the ritual shown – the transportation of statues – would have been a common occurrence, despite being seldom depicted. A man pours liquid in front of the statue, which is pulled by men with ropes. An officiant attaches a collar to the statue, illustrating entreaties in texts on contemporary statues for passers-by to fasten 'a garland at my neck'.

Statue of
Amenhotep I

c. 1295–1186 BCE

Limestone and paint • Height: 65 cm
(25 ⅝ in.), width: 27 cm (10 ⅝ in.)
From Deir el-Medina, Thebes, Egypt

EGYPTIAN MUSEUM,
TURIN, ITALY

King Amenhotep I (*c.* 1525–1504 BCE)
was venerated as the founder of the
village of Deir el-Medina, which
housed the workers who constructed
the royal tombs in the Valley of the
Kings. Amenhotep and his mother,
Queen Ahmose-Nefertari, were akin
to local patron saints of the craftsmen's
community. Texts from the village
record the statue of Amenhotep
being asked questions, in the manner
of an oracle. The style of this statue
dates it into the Ramesside period,
long after the legendary king's
death. It was likely housed in
a small, communal chapel
beside the village.

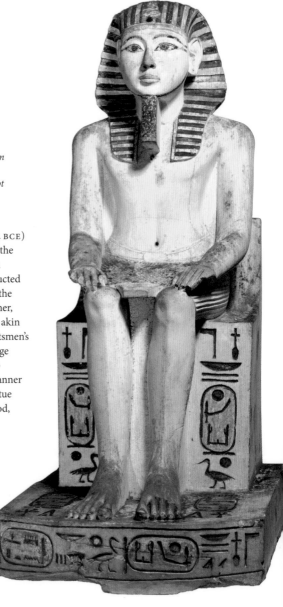

Ear stela

c. 1400 – 1200 BCE

Limestone • Height: 22.3 cm (8 ¾ in.),
width: 17.1 cm (6 ⅝ in.)
From Memphis, Egypt

BRITISH MUSEUM,
LONDON, UK

In ancient Egypt carving an object in stone was believed to make it magically effective. As a means of contacting the gods therefore, it was deemed expedient to carve ears on votive monuments to enable the gods to better hear the prayers carved upon them or, perhaps more commonly, spoken before them. This example bears forty-four human ears and carries a prayer to the god Ptah, 'lord of truth who hears petitions' – a form of the god believed to be particularly approachable for ordinary people. The stela was dedicated by a craftsman named Mahuia, who may have had a hand in carving the piece himself.

Ancestor bust

c. 1295–1186 BCE

*Limestone • Height: 51 cm (20 ⅛ in.), width:
26 cm (10 ¼ in.), depth: 29 cm (11 ⅜ in.) • From
Thebes, Egypt*

BRITISH MUSEUM, LONDON, UK

Everyday religious practice for most Egyptians
is likely to have involved ancestor worship,
especially in the home. Evidence of such
domestic ritual is poorly preserved, although
a number of limestone busts from the New
Kingdom town of Deir el-Medina and elsewhere
have been interpreted as images of venerated
ancestors. This example is very unusual in
having an inscription, for a woman called
Muteminet; most busts are uninscribed and
seem therefore to have acted as vessels for
several ancestral spirits. Muteminet's curled wig
is perhaps an allusion to Hathor, the goddess
of the west who welcomed the deceased.

Stela of Mose

c. 1279–1213 BCE

*Limestone • Height: 67.5 cm (26 ⅝ in.),
width: 50.5 cm (19 ⅞ in.), depth: 12.5 cm (4 ⅞ in.)
From Qantir, Egypt*

ROEMER-UND PELIZAEUS-MUSEUM,
HILDESHEIM, GERMANY

It is often unclear if the scenes that appear
on stelae depict generic ideals or historical
events. This stela has a sense of a particular
occasion because of the unusual details
shown. In the top left, the pharaoh (Ramesses
II) is shown worshipping the god Ptah; to the
right he scatters rewards from a cushioned
window ledge and in the lower scene he is
rewarding soldiers. Interestingly, the lower
scene has the king 'atop' a colossal statue
of himself, identified as 'Re-of Rulers'. The
intention may be to depict the king standing
at a balcony in a temple, near his colossus.

Mummy mask of Satdjehuty

c. 1500 BCE
Linen, plaster, gold and paint • Height: 61 cm (24 in.),
width: 32.5 cm (12 ¾ in.), depth: 19 cm (7 ½ in.)
Most likely from Thebes, Egypt

BRITISH MUSEUM, LONDON, UK

In a mythological episode, the weary sun god is
described as having bones of silver, hair of lapis
lazuli and flesh of gold. This divine nature – albeit
in depleted form – was what every Egyptian who
could afford it wished to imitate. Coffins and masks
of the wealthy use gold to liken themselves to the
untarnishability of the gods. This finely gilded mask
is for a woman of high rank, her gender indicated by
a vulture headdress over a striped wig. The name of
the deceased is not preserved on the plaster tab at the
bottom; however, based on links with other objects it
must be a noblewoman named Satdjehuty.

Bag of natron

c. 1327 BCE
Linen and natron • Height: 3.6 cm
(1 ⅜ in.), width: 6.6 cm (2 ⅝ in.),
length: 8.5 cm (3 ⅜ in.) • From the
Valley of the Kings, Thebes, Egypt

METROPOLITAN MUSEUM OF ART,
NEW YORK CITY, USA

The key to preserving a corpse in a hot country like Egypt was effective dehydration. Artificial mummification relied on the use of a substance called natron, a naturally occurring mixture of sodium carbonate and sodium chloride. During the embalming of the pharaoh's corpse, care was taken to preserve any detritus from the process – including natron that might have absorbed fluid from the semi-divine body. This bag of natron comes from a collection of materials used in the embalming of King Tutankhamun, which was not discarded but carefully buried near the royal tomb in the Valley of the Kings.

Chariot of Yuya

c. 1390 – 1352 BCE

Wood, gold and leather • Width of body: 90 cm (35 ½ in.), length of pole: 2 m (6 ½ ft), diameter of wheels: 75 cm (29 ½ in.) • From the Valley of the Kings, Thebes, Egypt

EGYPTIAN MUSEUM,
CAIRO, EGYPT

The horse-drawn chariot was a piece of military equipment introduced into Egypt by the Hyksos from western Asia. The Egyptians mastered the new technology and produced their own lightweight chariots that proved valuable in giving them an upper hand against their neighbours during the Eighteenth Dynasty. The chariot was also an elite mode of transport used for hunting as well as warfare. Chariots were included in the tombs of New Kingdom pharaohs and some high officials. This vehicle comes from the almost-intact tomb of Amenhotep III's father-in-law, Yuya, who – aptly – held the title 'Master of the Horses'.

MUMMY MASK
OF TUTANKHAMUN

c. 1327 BCE

Gold, glass and semi-precious stones • Height: 54 cm (21 ¼ in.), width: 39.3 cm
(15 ½ in.), depth: 49 cm (19 ¼ in.) • From the Valley of the Kings, Thebes, Egypt

EGYPTIAN MUSEUM, CAIRO, EGYPT

The mummy mask of Tutankhamun is perhaps the
most iconic object to survive from ancient Egypt.
The king is depicted wearing the *nemes*-headdress,
its distinctive blue stripes contributing to the mask's
instantly recognizable appearance. Unusually, on
his brow the king wears both the standard cobra but
also a vulture; the pair likely represent the protective
sister goddesses Isis and Nephthys. When discovered
over the face of the mummy, the mask wore a long
ceremonial beard and three-string bead choker. The
so-called 'Spell for the Head of Mystery', from chapter
151 of the *Book of the Dead*, is inscribed in hieroglyphs
on the mask's shoulders. This text was intended to
ensure the mask's magical effectiveness in protecting
the vulnerable head of the deceased from evil forces.
The text also credits the mask with giving the deceased
the power of sight. Recent research has suggested that
the mask is a composite creation, made originally for a
(female) predecessor of Tutankhamun. The distinctive
facial features of Tutankhamun, although unlikely to
be a lifelike portrait, were added in gold of a slightly
different colour to the rest of the mask.

*When the British Egyptologist Howard
Carter prepared Tutankhamun's mask
for display in Cairo, he deliberately
did not reattach the king's ceremonial
beard because he felt it was not
aesthetically pleasing.*

Scene of mourning

c. 1350 – 1250 BCE
Limestone • Height: 43 cm (16 ⅞ in.),
width: 40 cm (15 ¾ in.) From Egypt
BIRMINGHAM MUSEUM AND
ART GALLERY, UK

Ancient Egyptian funerals were clamorous
occasions, and depictions of them in tombs break a
major rule of Egyptian artistic decorum by showing
overt emotion. This is a fragment that comes from
a larger scene depicting a funeral. It shows the
mummy of the deceased, stood upright at the ritual
climax of the burial – the 'Opening of the Mouth'.
This ceremony magically revitalized the senses
of the deceased for the afterlife. The deceased's
female relatives are shown tearing their hair
and throwing dust over their heads.

Sarcophagus of Seti I

c. 1294 – 1279 BCE
Alabaster • Length: 2.8 m (9 ⅛ ft),
width at shoulders: 1.1 m (3 ⅝ ft)
From the Valley of the Kings,
Thebes, Egypt

SIR JOHN SOANE'S MUSEUM,
LONDON, UK

This sarcophagus was discovered by the Italian explorer Giovanni Battista Belzoni in October 1817 in the largest royal tomb in the Valley of the Kings. Only the basin, or trough, of the sarcophagus survives intact, although broken fragments of the lid – presumably destroyed by tomb robbers – were found alongside it. The translucent alabaster is incised and filled with 'Egyptian blue' or powdered blue frit. The decoration consists of finely executed scenes from the *Book of Gates*, describing the passage through the underworld of both the sun and the deceased king. A protective image of the sky goddess Nut appears on the base.

Shabti figures of Seti I

c. 1294 – 1279 BCE

Wood and resin • Height variable: c. 12 cm (4 ¾ in.) • From the Valley of the Kings, Thebes, Egypt

LOUVRE, PARIS, FRANCE

Despite an anticipated afterlife in the company of the gods, even kings were provided with shabti (servant) figurines. King Seti I was provided with more than any other king of Egypt, with estimates of over 1,000 examples. His shabtis were made of faience, steatite and alabaster, but the most common material was resin-covered wood – identified in some examples as juniper – often of rather mediocre workmanship. When the Italian explorer Giovanni Battista Belzoni discovered Seti I's tomb in 1817, he described finding hundreds of the figurines which, due to their quantity and flammability, he used as torches for light.

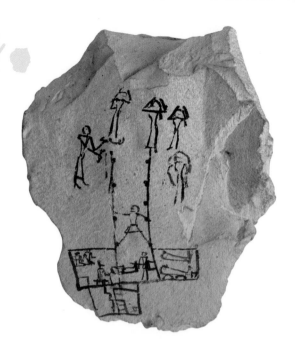

Ostracon depicting a funeral

c. 1450 – 1150 BCE
Limestone and black ink • Height: 11.2 cm (4 ⅜ in.),
width: 10.2 cm (4 in.) • From western Thebes, Egypt
MANCHESTER MUSEUM, UK

Ostraca were the ancient Egyptian equivalent of 'Post-it' notes – brief jottings on stone or pottery that were frequently discarded shortly after use. These were particularly common at the workmen's village of Deir el-Medina, and this ostracon is likely to be from there. The sketch it carries is unique in showing a funeral taking place. Four female mourners (with hands to their heads) and a male officiant stand by a tomb shaft, in which a man uses footholds to ascend or descend. In the chamber beneath, men (one wearing a jackal mask) carry a mummy to join at least two others alongside other tomb goods.

Egypt's Silver Age

Brightly painted wooden stelae are among the few items regularly included in Third Intermediate period elite graves. These associate the deceased with solar gods Re-Horakhty and Atum. Here a woman called Taperet adores the god Atum.

The decline of the New Kingdom in the late Twentieth Dynasty resulted in another return to regionalization for Egypt. The successors of the Ramesside kings continued to reside in the Delta, but a change in the course of the Nile led to the relocation of much of the great city of Pi-Ramesses north-eastwards to the site of Tanis. In the process, many monumental sculptures were transported. This enormous undertaking symbolizes an important characteristic of Third Intermediate period culture: a 'Silver Age', overshadowed by an illustrious past and obliged to reuse and ritually reactivate it.

After the death of Ramesses XI, Egypt remained notionally united under his successor, the Delta-based king named Smendes. In reality, power in the south was held by the Theban priesthood. Karnak was at the heart of a Theban theocratic state where the god Amun was the ruler, but the High Priest of Amun implemented his wishes. A dynasty of high priests emerged who presented themselves as kings. Among their most notable undertakings, they were responsible for the reburial of dozens of royal family

Tanis is home to an impressive collection of ruins – so much so that it featured as a location in the film Raiders of the Lost Ark (1981). Most of the sculpture belonged to earlier kings and was reused and deposited there during the Third Intermediate period.

members, dispossessed of their tombs in the Valley of the Kings. This process was motivated as much by economic need as by pious reverence for their illustrious ancestors, as there is plentiful evidence for the careful stripping of precious metals during the 'renovation' of coffins and re-wrapping of mummies.

Contemporary anxiety regarding the security of tombs motivated the concentration of northern royal burials within the temple precinct of the god Amun at Tanis. This move is mirrored in elite burial practices in general during the Third Intermediate period. Increasingly, individuals and family groups were laid to rest in unmarked tombs, often in reused sepulchres of some antiquity and usually associated with temples. In a parallel development, temples became the main (supposedly secure) setting for elite statuary, as construction of major tomb chapels almost entirely ceased. Elite monuments place particular emphasis on priestly pedigree and as a result much genealogical information survives from family trees recorded during this period.

The design of coffins changed to reflect an increased emphasis on the body and its container, rather than the tomb chapel as an arena for display. Partly due to economic constraints, the deceased was frequently buried in an older, reused coffin – often with subtle amendments to make it ritually suitable for a new owner. Coffin decoration became markedly more dense, while mummification attained its technical height in terms of preservation of the flesh; lace-up cartonnage mummy cases also increased in popularity at this time, fulfilling the same aim of creating a durable, defensive carapace for the deceased to survive eternity. A small number of objects – including canopic jars, shabtis and Ptah-Sokar-Osiris figurines – were provided as part of a standard funerary 'set'. Other extraneous objects of the type known from the New Kingdom and earlier are hardly attested.

The most important political shift during the Third Intermediate period occurred with the arrival of the Twenty-second Dynasty of kings of Libyan origin, who – in the person of Sheshonq I – were able to reunite Egypt and campaign actively in the Near East in the manner of Eighteenth and Nineteenth Dynasty kings. From their base at Tanis, the Libyan kings were able to control the south through key priestly appointments at Thebes, and were responsible for a resurgence in building work at Karnak. Again, there was a conspicuous return to the past in artistic forms, especially emulating the heyday of the New Kingdom 'Golden Age'. Such reverence for the past even involved transporting giant granite sarcophagi from the open and plundered royal tombs in the Valley of the Kings to Tanis. The spectacular discovery of the tombs of certain Twenty-second Dynasty royal burials at Tanis rivalled Tutankhamun's tomb in terms of the richness of their contents. The striking use of silver for coffins and other objects was an eloquent testimony to Egypt's 'Silver Age'. Alas, the timing of the discovery – in 1939 – meant it was eclipsed by the outbreak of World War II.

As the central power of the Libyan kings waned, so Egypt once again fragmented into smaller, autonomous polities governed by a variety of local rulers. This was the situation met by the invading army from Kush, far to the south of Egypt, in the Twenty-fifth Dynasty.

Reuse of royal sculpture included some of the most impressive sculptures at Karnak temple. Here, in the main outer courtyard, a colossal standing statue of Ramesses II was usurped by the Twenty-first Dynasty High Priest-King Pinudjem I and his wife.

Lotus cup

c. 840–731 BCE
Faience • Height: 14.5 cm (5 ¾ in.)
From Egypt
EGYPTIAN MUSEUM,
BERLIN, GERMANY

Bright blue, fluted, faience cups
are typical of the Third Intermediate
period and are often called 'chalices',
although any association with the Christian
Eucharist is unintended. Any specific ritual
function they might have had is unclear,
although they could have served a practical
purpose as a drinking vessel. The cups are
characterized by delicate, raised relief depicting
riverine scenes, gods or the pharaoh. Here,
divine motifs dominate, including the goddess
Hathor and dwarf god Bes. Hathor's
association with drunkenness may
explain her appearance on such
a vessel; the other gods provided
more general benefits to the drinker.

Bracelet with the Eye of Horus

c. 890 BCE

Gold, lapis lazuli, carnelian and white faience
Height: 4.6 cm (1 ¾ in.), width: 7 cm (2 ¾ in.)
From Tanis, Egypt

EGYPTIAN MUSEUM, CAIRO, EGYPT

Although found on the mummy of King Sheshonq II, this bracelet carries the name of his more illustrious predecessor Sheshonq I, and so may have been a family heirloom. The 'Eye of Horus' motif symbolizes 'wholeness' or 'completeness'. Paired with the chequered basket symbol for 'all' or 'every', the signs can therefore be read hieroglyphically as assuring 'all wholeness' for the king. This was to be a vain hope for Sheshonq II, as the king's mummy had almost completely decayed due to the wet Nile Delta environment of the royal tombs at Tanis.

Necklace spacer

c. 945–715 BCE
Faience • Height: 3.3 cm (1 ¼ in.),
width: 0.6 cm (¼ in.), length:
5.5 cm (2 ⅛ in.) • Most likely
from Tuna el-Gebel, Egypt

BRITISH MUSEUM, LONDON, UK

With a hole for suspension, this spacer
was to be strung on a necklace next to
other amulets. The composition shows
a deity grasping a captive, flanked by
two representations of Montu, the
god associated with warfare and thus
shown holding curved swords, along
with the lioness-headed Sekhmet
(left) and Mut (right). While such
divine scenes are common on temple
walls, the tiny scale of this openwork
faience – especially typical of the
Third Intermediate period – shows
technical skill in production.

Hyksos sphinx reused by Psusennes I

inscription: *c.* 1039–991 BCE,
sculpture: *c.* 1831–1786 BCE
*Granodiorite • Height: 1.5 m (4 ⅞ ft),
length: 2.3 m (7 ½ ft) • From Tanis, Egypt*
EGYPTIAN MUSEUM, CAIRO, EGYPT

The Twenty-first Dynasty is remarkable for a lack of royal sculpture. Economic considerations and perhaps a specific reverence for – or need to be associated with – the past motivated kings to reuse the works of earlier rulers. This imposing sculpture was first carved *c.* 1831–1786 BCE during the reign of the renowned Middle Kingdom king Amenemhat III, who is identifiable by the distinctive features of many of his statues. The king is shown as a sphinx with full lion's mane. The imposing, aggressive appearance of the sculpture was perhaps the reason that it had been reused at least three times before Psusennes I requisitioned the piece.

Relief block of Osorkon II

c. 874–850 BCE
*Granite • Height: 1 m (3 ¼ ft), width: 1.1 m (3 ¾ ft)
From Bubastis, Egypt*
PENN MUSEUM, PHILADELPHIA, USA

The royal 'heb-sed' festival or jubilee was a ritual of rejuvenation usually celebrated after the king had reigned for thirty years. This scene is only one part of a much larger, monumental gateway decorated with various episodes from the jubilee of King Osorkon II. As Osorkon seems to have only been on the throne for twenty-four years, the celebration is either fictional or was held early. Here the king strides forwards holding the crook and flail, the traditional sceptres of kingship, and wearing an enveloping cloak associated with the ritual throughout the pharaonic period. Standard-bearers and other ritualists stand before the monarch.

Plaque of Iuput II

c. 731–720 BCE

Faience • Height: 29.5 cm (11 ⅝ in.), width: 16 cm (6 ¼ in.)
From Egypt

NATIONAL MUSEUMS SCOTLAND, EDINBURGH, UK

This plaque was likely to have been used as an inlay for a wooden shrine. The crouching figure probably represents a little-known Delta-based king called Iuput II. He is shown in the guise of a child-god, naked and with his finger to his mouth as a sign of infancy. He emerges from a lotus flower, a mythological reference to the sun god appearing on the mound of creation. On the king's head, he wears a striped *nemes*-headdress and an elaborate, tall crown composed of plant fibres. The flail he holds in one hand is a sign of kingship. The discolouration suggests damage by fire.

Canopic coffinette

c. 890 BCE

Silver • Height: 25 cm (9 ⅞ in.) • From Tanis, Egypt
EGYPTIAN MUSEUM, CAIRO, EGYPT

Although most non-royal elites could expect their embalmed organs to be placed directly in a canopic container, the mummified entrails of kings from at least the reign of Tutankhamun were treated as if they were smaller versions of the king's complete mummy and placed in individual coffinettes. This miniature anthropoid coffin is one of four in beaten silver, an especially valuable material in ancient Egypt that was also used for the full-size coffin of King Sheshonq II. The coffinettes differ in that they have a human head with a *nemes*-headdress rather than the falcon head of the king's coffin.

BLOCK STATUE OF BASA

c. 945–715 BCE

*Limestone and paint • Height: 41 cm (16⅛ in.), width: 23 cm (9 in.),
depth: 20 cm (7⅞ in.) • From Dendera, Egypt*

ORIENTAL INSTITUTE, CHICAGO, USA

Ancient Egyptians were very proud of their heritage. Monuments
commemorating family lineage were particularly important during
the Third Intermediate period, and may have been influenced by
social practices originating with Egypt's rulers of Libyan origin. The
recording of genealogies was, however, a well-known Egyptian
practice and was often invoked to demonstrate and legitimize
priestly rights because temple staff could pass their offices – and
therefore benefits – down to the next generation of their families.

The block statue form – showing a man cloaked and with
his knees drawn up to his chin – offered an extensive flat surface
area to record lengthy inscriptions. Basa's inscription tells us
that he was a priest of Hathor, whose cult was centred on the
site of Dendera, where the statue was found and where there
now stands a Ptolemaic temple in her honour. Basa includes
a remarkable genealogy detailing no fewer than twenty-six
generations of his family. He was even able to trace his ancestry
back to Nebwenenef, a historically well-attested High Priest
of Amun during the reign of Ramesses II, several centuries
before Basa was born.

*The site of Dendera is now
dominated by a temple of
Ptolemaic date but this was
built on top of structures
associated with the worship
of Hathor that date back
to the Old Kingdom.*

Statue of Padiaset

inscription and relief:
c. 945–715 BCE; sculpture:
c. 1850–1750 BCE

*Greywacke • Height: 30.5 cm (12 in.),
width: 10.2 cm (4 in.), depth: 11.5 cm
(4 ½ in.) • From Egypt*

WALTERS ART MUSEUM,
BALTIMORE, USA

We do not know the name of the man who originally commissioned this statue, but we know that he discharged the important function of vizier (or chief minister) due to his distinctive costume. Perhaps it was this distinguished garment that attracted a man named Padiaset about a millennium later to pick out this sculpture for his own use. The piece is clearly late Middle Kingdom in style, but the formulation of the man's name (Padiaset means 'gift-of-Isis') and the arrangement of the texts and images, notably the figures of gods, indicate that these features were added during the Third Intermediate period.

Statuette of Amun

c. 945–715 BCE
*Gold • Height: 17.5 cm (6 ⅞ in.), width: 4.7 cm
(1 ⅞ in.), depth: 5.8 cm (2 ¼ in.) • From Egypt*
METROPOLITAN MUSEUM OF ART,
NEW YORK CITY, USA

The worship of the god Amun emerged in the
early Middle Kingdom at Karnak, where he rose
to become the principal state god in the New
Kingdom, and by the Third Intermediate period
another major temple to him was built at Tanis in
the north. This solid gold statuette may be a rare
survival of one of the god's cult images – a focal
point of worship – in one of those temples. Amun
wears his distinctive crown and holds a curved
sword, symbolizing military might, and the
sign of life. The facial features are typically
Twenty-second Dynasty in style, and echo
Eighteenth Dynasty models.

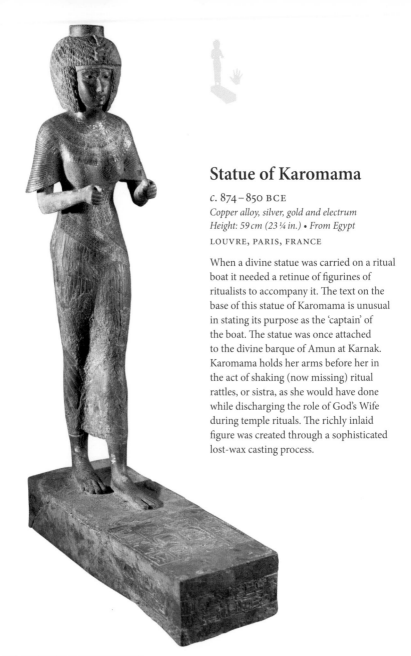

Statue of Karomama

c. 874–850 BCE
Copper alloy, silver, gold and electrum
Height: 59 cm (23 ¼ in.) • *From Egypt*
LOUVRE, PARIS, FRANCE

When a divine statue was carried on a ritual
boat it needed a retinue of figurines of
ritualists to accompany it. The text on the
base of this statue of Karomama is unusual
in stating its purpose as the 'captain' of
the boat. The statue was once attached
to the divine barque of Amun at Karnak.
Karomama holds her arms before her in
the act of shaking (now missing) ritual
rattles, or sistra, as she would have done
while discharging the role of God's Wife
during temple rituals. The richly inlaid
figure was created through a sophisticated
lost-wax casting process.

Amulet of Herishef

c. 818 – 715 BCE

*Gold • Height: 6 cm (2 ⅜ in.), width: 0.7 cm
(¼ in.), depth: 1.7 cm (⅝ in.) • From Herakleopolis
Magna, Egypt*

MUSEUM OF FINE ARTS, BOSTON, USA

The ram-headed god Herishef (meaning
'he who is upon his lake') had a cult centre
at Herakleopolis Magna. This tiny, cast gold
amulet was discovered by the archaeologist
W. M. Flinders Petrie under a pavement
of the temple there; so exceptional was the
piece that rather than donate it to a museum
Petrie offered it for sale. An inscription
names a king called Neferkara Peftjawybast,
recorded elsewhere as having collaborated
with the invading Nubian army of the later
Twenty-fifth Dynasty. The superior quality
of this piece suggests that it belonged to a
high-status individual, perhaps royalty, who
sought the protection of the local god.

SHABTI OF PINUDJEM I

c. 1070 – 1032 BCE
Faience • Height: 11.7 cm (4 ⅝ in.), width: 3.9 cm (1 ½ in.)
From Deir el-Bahri, Thebes, Egypt

BRITISH MUSEUM, LONDON, UK

Shabti figurines evolved from being considered substitutes of the deceased to being viewed as servants who would undertake agricultural tasks in the afterlife for their owner at the behest of the gods. Although the origin of the term shabti is debated, during the Twenty-first Dynasty the word was spelt ushabti and related to the verb *wesheb,* meaning 'to answer'. These 'answerers' were divided into 365 mummiform 'workers' provided with agricultural tools, one figure for each day of the year, and thirty-six 'overseers' – such as this one – who wear elite dress and hold whips instead of tools to control those ten workers under their command.

Pinudjem I and his family had a great interest in the past, and ordered the reburial of dozens of members of the New Kingdom royal family in their own family tomb at Deir el-Bahri. It is likely that those priests involved in moving these royal mummies observed the long outmoded use of bright blue faience for shabti figurines in earlier royal burials. It is intriguing to speculate that the distinctive 'Deir el-Bahri blue' was a deliberate echo of earlier royal funerary equipment.

Pinudjem's family and ancestors were buried in a large rock-cut tomb, referred to as DB 320. The extraordinary find was officially made in 1881, although it is likely that the tomb had been known – and gradually emptied – years earlier.

Funerary stela

c. 945–715 BCE
Wood and paint • Height: 27.5 cm (10 ⅞ in.), width:
17 cm (6 ¾ in.), depth: 3.8 cm (1 ½ in.) • Most likely
from Thebes, Egypt

LOUVRE, PARIS, FRANCE

During the Third Intermediate period, decorated
tomb walls were very rare. Decoration was instead
condensed onto the coffin and a small number of other
objects such as a brightly painted wooden stela. Here,
as was most common, the deceased is shown adoring
the god Re-Horakhty. This example belongs to a priest
of Amun named Renpetmaa. While it is not of the
highest quality and displays rather unsure hieroglyphic
calligraphy, this stela highlights what must have been
a mass production for the funerary industry. Perhaps it
was the work of an apprentice.

Mummy case

c. 945–715 BCE
Plaster, linen and paint • Height: 1.6 m (5 ¼ ft)
Most likely from Thebes, Egypt
ORIENTAL INSTITUTE, CHICAGO, USA

Cartonnage cases such as this are moulded from layers of linen (or papyrus) and plaster, formed around a mud and straw core. Once complete and while still pliable, the mummy would be inserted and laced up at the back like a corset. Widespread use of cartonnage was motivated by concerns about the security and integrity of the mummy rather than by economic factors, as cartonnage cases have been found within outer coffins made of more expensive wood. This inner casing belongs to a 'singer in the interior of the temple of Amun' at Karnak, called Meresamun.

Book of the Dead of Queen Nedjmet

c. 1080–1060 BCE

Papyrus and paint • Length: 4.1 m (13½ ft)
From Deir el-Bahri, Thebes, Egypt

BRITISH MUSEUM, LONDON, UK

The *Book of the Dead* is a modern name for a collection of spells known to the Egyptians by the more upbeat title, the *Book of Coming Forth by Day*. The book of spells, usually illustrated, was normally written on papyrus. This document provided both a passport and guidebook on the perilous journey to the afterlife, but also provided a guarantee of success – through knowledge of secret information – of getting into the kingdom of Osiris. Here, Queen Nedjmet is shown with her husband, the High Priest-turned-King Herihor, adoring Osiris at the 'weighing of the heart' judgment.

MODEL CANOPIC JARS

c. 945–715 BCE

Limestone • Average height: 24.1 cm (9 ½ in.), average diameter:
13.6 cm (5 ⅜ in.) • Most likely from western Thebes, Egypt

MUSEUM OF FINE ARTS, BOSTON, USA

Changes in conceptions of the body during the Third Intermediate period placed greater importance on the integrity of the mummy within its coffin, and the widespread experience of violent tomb robbery demonstrated how vulnerable extraneous elements like canopic jars could be. It therefore became common practice in this period for the mummified internal organs to be replaced back within the chest cavity of the corpse, which rendered canopic containers superfluous. Yet the Egyptians seemed loathe to dispense with such a core item of funerary equipment, so they included solid model (or 'dummy') jars instead. These represented the protective deities the Four Sons of Horus – Imsety (human), Qebehsenuef (falcon), Hapy (baboon) and Duamutef (jackal) – and ensured their continued protection of the deceased despite not serving their prior function as containers. These examples name each god in black paint, with an incised line to indicate the usual join between lid and jar. Many excavated examples of such model jars have been found in the large Third Intermediate period cemetery in the vicinity of the Ramesseum, the mortuary temple of Ramesses II, and these jars may derive from that area.

The area surrounding the Ramesseum – the mortuary temple of King Ramesses II – was intensively used for burials of temple staff and their families during the Third Intermediate period.

Embalming plaque

c. 1069 – 945 BCE

*Wax • Height: 8.2 cm (3 ¼ in.),
length: 10.2 cm (4 in.) • From Egypt*

BRITISH MUSEUM, LONDON, UK

During the Third Intermediate period, the internal organs removed during embalming were often returned to the chest cavity rather than placed in canopic jars. The cut made by the embalmer's knife to remove the entrails – usually in the left flank – was a point of injury and thus vulnerability to negative forces for the corpse, and as such required sewing closed or being covered with an amuletic plaque like this one. In myth, the eye of the god Horus was injured by his evil uncle Seth but healed by his mother Isis. This 'wedjat' (meaning 'restored' or 'whole') eye was a powerful symbol of regeneration and healing.

Coffin of Prince Amenemhat

c. 1150–945 BCE
Wood and paint • Height: 35.1 cm (13⅞ in.),
width: 30.6 cm (12 in.), length: 1 m (3¼ ft)
From western Thebes, Egypt

METROPOLITAN MUSEUM OF ART,
NEW YORK CITY, USA

The reuse of coffins was widespread in ancient
times, especially during the Twenty-first Dynasty,
and has been the subject of detailed study by
Egyptologists. Economic circumstances and shifts in
burial customs during the early Third Intermediate
period meant that pressure built up on the supply of
funerary provisions, and tomb robbery was common.
This child-sized coffin, dating to around the end of the
New Kingdom, has been reused by removing some of
the hieroglyphs on the lid and replacing them with the
name of a royal prince, Amenemhat, whose parentage
is uncertain. The identity of the coffin's original
occupant is unknown.

Egypt in an International Age

The Ptolemies continued many of the monumental projects of the last native Egyptian kings, the Thirtieth Dynasty. This sphinx sits at Alexandria, the Greek-facing capital of the Ptolemies, but owes much to the native style of rendering the royal visage.

Ancient Kush, centred on the Fourth Cataract of the Nile in what is modern Sudan, had been systematically oppressed by the Egyptians for centuries. While Egypt fragmented during the Third Intermediate period, the Kushite state had flourished. A ruler named Piankhi led an army north and, in his Victory Stela, gives one of the most detailed accounts of a military expedition to survive from the ancient world. In some sense this was a holy war, as the Kushites particularly honoured their local form of the god Amun, and presented themselves as more Egyptian than the Egyptians. The activities of the Kushite Twenty-fifth Dynasty are best known from evidence in the south of Egypt, unsurprisingly focused on Karnak, the original home of their patron deity Amun.

The arrival of the Kushites heralded an extended period of foreign domination: Nubians, Assyrians, Persians, Greeks and Romans would rule Egypt for most of the next millennium. These cultures brought with them new influences that are reflected in the often surprisingly multicultural nature of surviving evidence from Egypt at this time. Kushite rulers, for example, combined traditional depictions of Egyptian kingship with innovative forms of regalia to present themselves as legitimate pharaohs: an exercise in propaganda that would be employed by different invaders for several centuries afterwards.

Kushite rule in Egypt lasted for almost a century and was ended by the geopolitical manoeuvrings of the Assyrian Empire, which ousted the Twenty-fifth Dynasty and established in their place an Egyptian vassal based at the Delta town of Sais. These Saite vassals soon overthrew the yoke of Assyrian rule and, under King Psamtek I, re-established Egypt as a united kingdom. Egypt now also boasted a formidable military force, having co-opted Greek mercenaries and developed a significant naval presence to compete with other powers in the eastern Mediterranean.

More than at any other period, during the Twenty-fifth and Twenty-sixth Dynasties there was a very conscious return to already ancient models in texts, artistic depictions and architecture. A large number of non-royal temple monuments survive, particularly statuary, with the intent of showing the eternal piety of their donors. Individuals

The Ptolemaic period saw the melding of a rich variety of cultural elements. Nowhere is this more evident than at the tomb of the nobleman Petosiris at Tuna el-Gebel in Middle Egypt. His tomb chapel has the appearance of a small Egyptian temple, but has inside an eclectic mix of Greek and Egyptian styles.

Alexander the Great presented himself as Egypt's liberator from Persian tyranny. This mosaic dates to a couple of centuries after Alexander's death, and was located on the floor in the House of the Faun at Pompeii. It is now in the Naples Archaeological Museum in Italy.

of the highest elite could commission several statues of themselves along with impressive monumental tombs in western Thebes and in the Memphite necropolis. Many of these provide extensive inscriptions, from which incidental historical information can be gleaned.

The impact of the invasion of Cambyses in 525 BCE reverberated in the realm of funerary iconography with the appearance of Persian features. Relatively brief spells of independence from Persian rule saw Egypt governed by a native dynasty, the Thirtieth according to the historian Manetho, ending in Nectanebo II – the last native ruler of Egypt for over 2,000 years. This dynasty harked back to the Saite period, and championed major building works that continued in the following decades. After another brutal Persian influx, Egypt was emphatically 'liberated' by the Macedonian general Alexander the Great. His successors were a family of kings called Ptolemy, who lived very much as Greeks, based at the new coastal capital of Alexandria. This was despite the fact that they were shown in countless temple reliefs throughout the country discharging the traditional functions of a pharaoh. The last Ptolemy was in fact a woman, an Egyptian-speaker named Cleopatra VII, and with her death in 30 BCE Egypt was absorbed into the Roman Empire.

Throughout the Late period, the funerary industry continued to supply significant demand and it is fair to say that the majority of surviving pharaonic mortuary evidence comes from the last centuries BCE. Whether this represents a greater proportion of society benefiting from the industry, or simply better preservation, is difficult to say. While tombs appear increasingly to have been communal, preparations for the afterlife were still an elaborate undertaking for the wealthiest. With time, traditional components of burials – such as canopic jars and shabtis – went out of fashion. In the last centuries BCE, a vast religious industry in mummified animals swept the country and attracted pilgrims from abroad to purchase and dedicate the mummies as gifts for the gods. This focus on traditional pharaonic animal forms of divinity may represent a surge of nationalism in the face of foreign rule.

Signet ring

c. 664–525 BCE
Gold • Diameter: 3 cm (1 ⅛ in.),
length of bezel: 3.4 cm (1 ⅜ in.)
From Egypt

BRITISH MUSEUM, LONDON, UK

Inscribed rings such as this identified the name and title(s) of their owner; the bezel could be pressed into clay to seal documents or other commodities. This ring belonged to a man called Sheshonq, a name of Libyan origin, who held the title 'Chief Steward of the Divine Adoratrice'. He is likely the same individual who owned an impressive tomb in the Assasif region of Thebes. The Chief Steward was an official with oversight of a considerable estate, administering the lands and possessions of the Divine Adoratrice (or 'God's Wife') – a leading religious figure at the time.

Assyrian helmet

c. 690 – 664 BCE
Copper alloy • Height: 21 cm (8 ¼ in.) • From Thebes, Egypt
MANCHESTER MUSEUM, UK

In 664 BCE the ancient city of Thebes – cult centre
of the great god Amun – was sacked by an invading
Assyrian army sent by King Ashurbanipal, driving
the Nubian rulers of Egypt back to their homeland.
This metal helmet, found by the archaeologist W.
M. Flinders Petrie during excavations of temples
on the Theban west bank, attests to events of
the time. Assyrian reliefs depict soldiers of
the Neo-Assyrian Empire wearing the same
distinctively pointed helmet, and several
examples of iron and other metals are
known. The conical shape deflected
blows but would have been hot
to wear in battle.

Ram's-head amulet

c. 750 – 664 BCE
*Gold • Height: 4.2 cm (1 ⅝ in.), width: 3.6 cm
(1 ⅜ in.), depth: 2 cm (¾ in.) • Most likely
from Sudan*

METROPOLITAN MUSEUM OF ART, NEW
YORK CITY, USA

Nubian pharaohs of the Twenty-fifth Dynasty
especially venerated a form of the god Amun
who often took the guise of a ram. New
Kingdom pharaohs Amenhotep III and
Ramesses II had themselves depicted in their
Nubian temples with ram's horns as a sign of
their heightened divinity in these contexts.
Ram's horns may be a borrowing from earlier
ideologies. Depictions of Nubian kings show
them with jewelry hung around their necks
featuring the heads of rams. This object may
be a rare survival of this type of royal jewelry.

Recarved royal head

c. 716 – 702 BCE
*Granite • Height: 97 cm (38 ¼ in.)
From Karnak, Egypt*

EGYPTIAN MUSEUM, CAIRO, EGYPT

Representations of Nubian kings of the
Twenty-fifth Dynasty almost always present
the pharaoh wearing a double cobra (or
'uraeus') on his brow, rather than the single
serpent. The symbolism of this innovation
may reflect the Nubians' perception of
themselves as Lords of Two Lands: not only
Upper and Lower Egypt, but both Egypt
and Nubia. This granite head was probably
originally carved for a New Kingdom ruler
(*c.* 1250–1150 BCE): the single uraeus has been
adapted by splitting it into two to make it an
appropriate depiction of the Nubian Shabaka,
whose name is carved on the back pillar.

Rosetta Stone

196 BCE

*Granodiorite • Height: 1.1 m (3 ⅝ ft), width: 75.7 cm (29 ¾ in.),
depth: 28.4 cm (11 ⅛ in.) • From El-Rashid, Egypt*

BRITISH MUSEUM, LONDON, UK

The so-called Rosetta Stone is one of the most iconic
museum pieces in the world. It describes a decree
passed by a council of priests, affirming the royal
cult of the thirteen-year-old Ptolemy V on the first
anniversary of his coronation. The stone's importance
lies in the fact that it has the same text written in three
different scripts: hieroglyphic and demotic Egyptian,
and Greek. As scholars in the early 1800s knew Greek,
it provided the key to deciphering the unknown
Egyptian scripts. The process of decipherment was
critically advanced by the Frenchman Jean-François
Champollion in 1822, based on the Rosetta Stone.

Statue of Cleopatra VII

c. 51–30 BCE

Black basalt • Height: 1m (3½ft) • From Egypt
STATE HERMITAGE MUSEUM,
ST PETERSBURG, RUSSIA

The famous Cleopatra was in fact the last of at least seven women with that name in the Ptolemaic Dynasty. She is shown here in the typically frontal pose of an Egyptian queen, yet with distinctively Ptolemaic curvaceousness. She grasps both Egyptian and Greek symbols: the *ankh* or hieroglyphic symbol for life, usually associated with pharaonic divinities, and the double cornucopia, or horn of plenty, associated with queens worshipped in the Greek ruler cult, illustrating Cleopatra's cosmopolitan outlook. Although the statue is not inscribed, the triple cobra – or uraeus – on her brow indicates that this is indeed Cleopatra VII.

Statue head of Ptolemy VIII

c. 170 – 116 BCE

Diorite • Height: 47 cm (18 ½ in.) • From Egypt

CINQUANTENAIRE MUSEUM, BRUSSELS, BELGIUM

Alexander the Great's successors on the throne of
Egypt were a Macedonian family of kings called
Ptolemy, who strove to appear as legitimate pharaohs
in Egyptian royal regalia. However, the traditional
double crown rarely appears as the sole royal
headgear in sculptures of the Ptolemaic rulers.
Here is an exception. Although the identity
of the king is not explicitly stated by
an inscription, many scholars have
pointed to the full face, wide-open
eyes and pouting, cupid's bow
lips as belonging to King Ptolemy
VIII, known as *Physcon* 'the fat'.
This life-size sculpture blends
the influence of both Greek
and Egyptian trends.

STATUETTE OF OSIRIS

c. 750 – 300 BCE

Wood, gold and copper alloy • Height: 57.2 cm (22 ½ in.) • From Egypt

LOS ANGELES COUNTY MUSEUM OF ART, USA

Osiris was one of the earliest and perhaps the most consistent divine presences in the ancient Egyptian pantheon. His associations with death, rebirth and fertility ensured his prominence throughout pharaonic history and beyond. The central Osiris myth concerns his death by drowning, and subsequent dismemberment by his jealous brother Seth. Through the magical ministrations of his wife, Isis, Osiris was brought back to life. This process became the divine antecedent for the ritual of mummification. Osiris is almost always shown as tightly wrapped in linen, holding symbols of kingship over the underworld.

As a god reborn, Osiris was the guarantor of a life after death. By the first millennium BCE, Osiris had become one of the most popular deities for the living to approach and he is often represented in statuary – from the most modest bronze figurines to impressive gilded images such as this. Originally inlaid and provided with (now missing) royal sceptres, this statuette was probably donated to a temple as a votive offering. The details of the donor would have been inscribed on a now-missing base. It is less likely, although not impossible, that this image could have been a focal point of ritual activity in a temple shrine.

One of the most frequently represented deities from ancient Egypt, Osiris commonly appears in funerary contexts as the key guarantor of a life after death. He is often shown with green skin, a marker of regeneration.

Relief fragment

747–690 BCE

*Sandstone and paint • Height: 49 cm (19¼ in.),
length: 63.4 cm (25 in.), depth: 18.5 cm (7¼ in.)
From western Thebes, Egypt*

ORIENTAL INSTITUTE, CHICAGO, USA

Thebes during the Twenty-fifth and
Twenty-sixth Dynasties was essentially
ruled by a woman: the God's Wife (or
Divine Adoratrice) of Amun. Discharging
the most important religious role in Egypt
after the pharaoh, she appears even to have
eclipsed the male High Priest of Amun in
significance. With her own land holdings,
administered by a staff of officials, she also
headed a group of female singers during
rituals. A woman named Diesehebsed is
shown here accompanying the God's Wife
Amenirdis, indicating her importance.
Diesehebsed came from one of the most
important families in Thebes at a time
when women were highly prominent
in religious life.

Shabaka Stone

c. 716 – 702 BCE

*Basalt • Height: 66 cm (26 in.), length:
1.3 m (4¼ ft) • From Memphis, Egypt*

BRITISH MUSEUM, LONDON, UK

The Egyptians had a number of beliefs about the
creation of the universe, which appear to have been
held concurrently. Perhaps the most philosophical
account by modern standards is the so-called
Memphite Theology, which is preserved on this stone
slab. The text describes the creation of the universe by
Ptah, who conceived of things in his 'heart' and spoke
them with his mouth to bring them into existence.
Although the text was once thought to date to the
Pyramid Age, the inscription clearly names King
Shabaka of the Twenty-fifth Dynasty, who claims to
have discovered the text on a 'worm-eaten' papyrus
and had it copied.

Statuette of Imhotep

c. 750 – 525 BCE
Copper alloy, gold and silver • Height: 17.6 cm
(6 ⅞ in.) • From Egypt

MUSEUM OF FINE ARTS,
BUDAPEST, HUNGARY

Despite the sinister connotations of the name
'Imhotep' in modern Hollywood movies,
the historical Imhotep was one of the few
mortals to attain divine status after his death.
He is chiefly associated with the builder of
the Step Pyramid, King Djoser, under whom
he served in a variety of capacities as priest,
astronomer and overseer of craftsmen.
He later earned a reputation as a sage
and patron of scribes. By the Late period
Imhotep was venerated as a healer, the
son of the god Ptah, and was most often
shown as here – wearing a skullcap and
seated with a papyrus roll on his lap.

Osiris brick

c. 750–300 BCE

*Pottery • Length: 22.5 cm (8 ⅞ in.),
width: 13.5 cm (5 ⅜ in.) • From
western Thebes, Egypt*

MEDITERRANEAN MUSEUM,
STOCKHOLM, SWEDEN

The ancient Egyptian calendar was closely connected to the rhythms of the seasons. In the first millennium BCE, the popularity and associations of the god Osiris had spread beyond the afterlife to encompass fertility as well as regeneration. In this context, he was linked with the yearly Nile flood. At the annual festival of Khoiak, fired pottery bricks such as this – with the silhouette of Osiris impressed upon them – were filled with soil, planted with seeds and swathed in linen. The area of Medinet Habu on the Theban west bank seems to have been a focal point for this ritual activity.

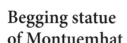

Begging statue
of Montuemhat

c. 680–630 BCE

*Granite • Height: 50 cm (19 ⅝ in.)
From Karnak, Thebes, Egypt*

EGYPTIAN MUSEUM,
CAIRO, EGYPT

Montuemhat was the Mayor of Thebes, and could afford numerous statues of himself, of which over a dozen are now known. At first sight, this sculpture may appear unflattering, yet it is of a special New Kingdom type representing the individual with a balding head and a hand cupped to the mouth (which is not preserved here). These so-called 'begging' statues were a means of associating the deceased with the goddess Hathor. Inscriptions claim that the humble-looking statue owner is able to pass on the prayers of pilgrims to the goddess. It was hoped that in return passers-by would pour a liquid offering for the statue to 'drink'.

Jackal mummy

c. 750–300 BCE

Linen and animal remains • Height: 34 cm (13 ⅜ in.),
width: 10 cm (3 ⅞ in.) • Most likely from Saqqara, Egypt

ORIENTAL MUSEUM, DURHAM, UK

Jackals were sacred to Anubis, the god associated with mummification. This attractive jackal mummy would have been an appropriate gift for the god, although its appearance belies what is inside. The head is formed mostly of linen and the 'body' consists of broken bones, possibly canine but perhaps human too. About one third of animal mummies contain a complete animal, another third contain part of an animal and a final third contain no animal bones at all. As some of the most elaborate mummies have the least animal content, perhaps the intention of the gift was sufficient to appease the deity.

Statue of Tjaisetimu

c. 664–525 BCE

Limestone • Height: 1.2 m (3 ⅞ ft), width: 33.5 cm (13 ¼ in.)
Most likely from Giza, Egypt

BRITISH MUSEUM, LONDON, UK

Art and culture during the Twenty-sixth Dynasty are
well-known for their tendency to refer to the past.
This statue is notable because it so closely resembles
an Old Kingdom piece in material, stance and wig.
An inscription on the base describes the statue as a
'likeness', probably in reference to the older statues that
the sculptor was imitating rather than to the individual
represented by the statue. The owner, Tjaisetimu, was a
priest who officiated in the cult of royal statues, implying
he knew the proper ritual requirements of traditional
forms of temple sculpture such as this.

JACKAL MASK

c. 750 – 300 BCE

Linen, plaster and paint • Height: 24 cm (9 ½ in.),
width: 25 cm (9 ⅞ in.), depth: 36 cm (14 ⅛ in.) • From Egypt

ROYAL PUMP HOUSE MUSEUM, HARROGATE, UK

Ancient Egyptian ritual often involved the impersonation of
various deities by human actors. Ritualists could assimilate the
powers of a god by claiming to be them, and the easiest way
to do this was by wearing a mask. Despite the large number
of mummy masks that survive, this is one of very few preserved
examples of a mask worn by a living person. Made of a mixture
of linen and plaster known as cartonnage, this mask would
have been light enough to wear comfortably.

A key component of the funeral ceremony was the
'Opening the Mouth' ritual (see p.69), in which the
mummified body was stood upright. Using a series of ritual
implements, the senses of the deceased were magically
restored. This and other episodes of the funeral were
depicted as being conducted by the jackal-god Anubis.
The existence of objects such as this head-covering
imply that the scenes show a man wearing a mask
rather than an abstract ideal of the god's presence.

The god Anubis features in scenes of mummification and the funeral, as a guarantor of a safe passage through to the afterlife. Masks enabled humans to take on his divine identity during such rituals.

Ibis bird coffin

c. 664 – 30 BCE

Wood, gold, glass and copper alloy • Height: 31.8 cm (12½ in.), length: 47 cm (18½ in.) • From Egypt

BURRELL COLLECTION, GLASGOW, SCOTLAND, UK

The ibis bird was almost exclusively the sacred animal of Thoth, the god of wisdom and of writing. His long, curved beak was likened either to a crescent moon or – when observed by a riverbank – to a scribe's pen as it dips into ink. This figurine is both a statue of the sacred bird and a coffin, as it contains a sealed compartment – revealed by X-ray imaging – that was once intended to have contained some mummified material. As such, the splendid statue acted in the same way as other mummified animals, as a gift to appease the gods – particularly Thoth.

Stela for an Apis bull

547 BCE
Limestone • Height: 1.1 m (3½ ft),
width: 63.5 cm (25 in.), depth: 35 cm
(13¾ in.) • From Saqqara, Egypt

LOUVRE, PARIS, FRANCE

This epitaph was set up for the sacred Apis bull, believed to be an incarnation of the Memphite god Ptah. The pharaoh is shown kneeling before the bull, a sign of royal piety towards a living god. Somewhat like choosing the Dalai Lama, each bull would be selected upon the death of the previous one, based on a calf's special markings. Dated to the twenty-third year of the reign of King Amasis, this inscription records the death, mummification and burial of the bull. The precise dates given for the bull's birth and death provide key data for fixed points in time.

Votive sculptor's model

c. 400 – 200 BCE

Limestone • Height: 15.3 cm (6 in.), width: 17.2 cm (6 ¾ in.), depth: 2 cm (⅛ in.) • Most likely from Faiyum, Egypt

METROPOLITAN MUSEUM OF ART, NEW YORK CITY, USA

Egyptologists have puzzled over the meaning of a group of objects that seem to be preparatory studies for relief carvings or statues. Despite being finished objects in themselves, many depict the unfinished stages of a design. Many more of these Late period objects survive than earlier 'trial pieces' and the most plausible interpretation is that these are votive offerings, perhaps connected with the dedication of temples. The male figure depicted here has a side-lock and uraeus cobra on a skull cap. Most likely this represents a child god – either Harpocrates or Ihy.

Crocodile mummy

c. 650–550 BCE

Animal remains and resin
Length: 3.8 m (12½ ft) • From Kom Ombo, Egypt

BRITISH MUSEUM, LONDON, UK

Gods could take physical form on earth. The immense size of this reptile implies that it lived a long life rather than being dispatched relatively young to be donated as a votive offering by pilgrims. This may, therefore, be a rare example of a cult animal venerated as a physical manifestation of the god Sobek. Although some of the internal organs were removed in the mummification process, CT-scans showed that remaining contents of the stomach included a cow's shoulder and forearm bones, implying a rich diet for this god-on-earth. The resin-covered mummy also has twenty-five mummified baby crocodiles stuck to its back.

Healing statue

c. 400–300 BCE
Greywacke • Height: 67.7 cm (26 ⅝ in.)
From Egypt
LOUVRE, PARIS, FRANCE

This statue of a priest of Bastet was set up in a temple and shows a man holding a so-called 'Horus cippus', with a depiction of the innocent child-god Horus trampling – and thus triumphing over – dangerous beasts. The surface of the statue is almost completely covered with magical texts including spells to cure snake bites and scorpion stings. This example is explicit about its function: water poured over the statue would magically absorb the healing power of the hieroglyphic text and could be collected in a basin in order to be drunk or applied to the body.

Inscribed plaque

c. 100 BCE

*Siltstone • Height: 18.5 cm
(7 ¼ in.), width: 9.5 cm (3 ¾ in.)
From Meroë, Sudan*

WALTERS ART MUSEUM,
BALTIMORE, USA

Meroë was the capital of the kingdom of Kush to the
south of Egypt, excavated by the British archaeologist
John Garstang from 1909 to 1914. This plaque – probably
part of a stela – was discovered there. On one side (below
left) is depicted King Tanyidamani (*c.* 110–90 BCE);
on the reverse (below right) is the lion-headed god
Apedemak, the most important deity in the Nubian
pantheon, within whose temple the plaque was found.
The king wears a variation on an elaborate pharaonic
hemhem crown, distinctively Kushite earrings with
sun discs and rams' heads, and a patterned robe. The
inscriptions are written in cursive Meroitic script, which
is as yet undeciphered.

CAT MUMMIES

C. 300 BCE–100 CE

*Linen and animal remains • Heights: (left) 43 cm (14 ¾ in.), (right) 37.5 cm
(14 ¾ in.), widths: (left) 9.5 cm (3 ¾ in.), (right) 8 cm (3 ¼ in.) • From Egypt*

WORLD MUSEUM, LIVERPOOL, UK

Ancient Egypt is closely associated with the veneration of cats.
The Greek historian Herodotus mentions that the Egyptians
would shave off their eyebrows in mourning for a deceased
cat, which subsequently led to the misconception of the
Egyptians worshipping their 'pet' cats. In fact, the reality was
less sentimental. Mummified cats are attested in their thousands
from several sites in Egypt. Many that have been scientifically
imaged show juvenile cats within the wrappings, implying an
intense industry in the killing of felines. The purpose of this
slaughter was to supply votive offerings purchased and dedicated
by pilgrims to the cult of the goddess Bastet. Tall, skittle-shaped
mummies such as these specimens may have made them suitable
to stack for storage or sale. Temple staff would eventually gather
the mummies and bury them in underground catacombs.

In 1890, an incredible 180,000 cat mummies from catacombs
at Beni Hasan were shipped to the United Kingdom, first to act
as ballast on ships and then to be auctioned on the Liverpool
dockside for use as fertilizer. The use of 'Egyptian "fur-tiliser"'
was lampooned in periodicals such as *Punch* magazine, but
several examples such as these entered museums and became
popular exhibits.

*The site of Beni Hasan
is best known today for
its impressive rock-cut
Middle Kingdom tombs.
It was also home to
catacombs – perhaps
partly exploiting older
tomb structures, as at
Saqqara – filled with
thousands of cat mummies.*

Head of a bald man

c. 380 – 332 BCE

*Greywacke • Height: 10.5 cm (4 ⅛ in.), width: 8.5 cm (3 ⅜ in.),
depth: 11.3 cm (4 ½ in.) • Most likely from Saqqara, Egypt*

MUSEUM OF FINE ARTS, BOSTON, USA

Despite its appeal to modern aesthetics as an *objet d'art*, it is
doubtful that this head is a true-to-life portrait of a real person.
Its modern prestige largely derives from being detached from
its (probably much more generic) body. The lifelike face was
a means of attracting the attention of temple visitors.
Often referred to as the 'Boston Green Head',
this piece is one of a small number of Late
period 'portraits' of particularly striking
artistic quality. This head probably
derived from French excavations
at Saqqara and was once in the
possession of Prince Napoleon
Bonaparte and the collector
Edward Perry Warren.

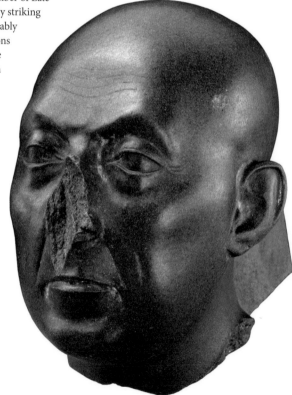

Harpocrates figurine

c. 150 BCE

*Terracotta and paint • Height: 14 cm
(5 ½ in.) • From Egypt*

MUSEUM OF FINE ARTS,
BUDAPEST, HUNGARY

The god Horus-the-child became popular
as Harpocrates in the Ptolemaic and Roman
periods. He is identifiable as a boy with
a finger to his mouth, a sign of infancy
in pharaonic art. In his arm he holds
a cornucopia, or 'horn of plenty'. The
most obvious survival from Egyptian
iconography is the representation of the
double crown – traditionally worn by
Horus in pharaonic depictions – upon
the head of Harpocrates. Such hollow
terracotta images survive in huge
numbers from Egypt and may have
been left as votives at temples or
displayed in household shrines.

Zodiac ceiling

c. 100 BCE
Sandstone • Length: 2.5 m (8 ¼ ft), width: 2.5 m (8 ¼ ft)
From Dendera, Egypt
LOUVRE, PARIS, FRANCE

The so-called Dendera Zodiac once formed part of
the ceiling of a small chapel of Osiris located on the
roof of the temple of Hathor at Dendera. It represents
a circular sky, held aloft by four women assisted by
falcon-headed spirits. Thirty-six spirits or 'decans'
around the circumference symbolize the 360 days
of the Egyptian year. The constellations include
the signs of the zodiac, mostly represented almost
as they are today. Aries, Taurus, Scorpio and
Capricorn, for example, are easily recognizable,
whereas others use pharaonic motifs: for example,
Aquarius is represented as Hapy, the god of the
Nile flood, pouring water from two vases.

Hypocephalus

664–525 BCE

Linen and plaster inscribed in ink
Diameter: 20 cm (7 ⅞ in.) • Most
likely from western Thebes, Egypt

ASHMOLEAN MUSEUM,
OXFORD, UK

A hypocephalus (literally, 'beneath the head') was an amuletic device intended to be placed under the head of the mummy. Hypocephali in the form of cartonnage discs were first produced in the Twenty-sixth Dynasty and are attested for several centuries thereafter. These discs are usually inscribed with Chapter 162 of the *Book of the Dead*, which was intended to 'warm' the head of the deceased. The intention was to liken the deceased to the sun god, illustrated here as a four-ram-headed entity; the shape of the circle also offered protection. This example was made for a woman named Tasheritenkhonsu.

Funerary cone

c. 680–630 BCE

Pottery • Length: 17.8 cm (7 ⅛ in.),
diameter: 8.1 cm (3 ¼ in.) • From
western Thebes, Egypt

LOS ANGELES COUNTY
MUSEUM OF ART, USA

During the New Kingdom at Thebes, it was common for elite tomb chapels to have a series of round-ended pottery cones inserted above their entrances, each stamped with the tomb owner's name and titles. This practice went out of fashion in the late New Kingdom but reappeared about the time of Montuemhat. Although he was an important individual – and was even referred to as the 'king of Thebes' by the Assyrians – he seems to have been most proud of a rather modest priestly title – 'Fourth Prophet of Amun' – which appears on most of his monuments, including his funerary cones.

Shabti of Taharqa

c. 690–664 BCE
*Serpentinite • Height: 34.2 cm (13 ½ in.),
width: 12.5 cm (4 ⅞ in.) • From Nuri, Sudan*
MUSEUM OF FINE ARTS, BOSTON, USA

One of the traditions reintroduced by the
kings of the Twenty-fifth Dynasty was the
habit of including large stone shabtis in
burials. The same practice was adopted by
wealthy officials at Thebes. This is one of
about 1,000 stone shabti figures that appear
to have been made in four sets, of different
materials, perhaps in different workshops.
Many carry markings on the feet, perhaps
to indicate their intended orientation once
set in place. The shabtis were discovered
in situ around the king's sarcophagus within
his pyramid. Unlike most representations of
Kushite kings, which have a double uraeus,
the shabtis of Taharqa have only one.

Sarcophagus of Pabasa

c. 664–525 BCE

Granite • Height: 1.2 m (3 ⅞ ft), width: 75 cm (29 ½ in.), length: 2.4 m (7 ⅞ ft) • From western Thebes, Egypt

KELVINGROVE ART GALLERY AND MUSEUM, GLASGOW, SCOTLAND, UK

The word 'sarcophagus' comes from the Greek for 'flesh eater', although the Egyptian conception of these stone containers was one of protecting the corpse rather than physically consuming it. The style of this example references elite sarcophagi of the New Kingdom, and perhaps it is a reused older piece. Pabasa was a Chief Steward of the God's Wife of Amun and his is the best preserved sarcophagus from a group of large tombs belonging to his colleagues and contemporaries. Alexander, Duke of Hamilton, brought two sarcophagi from Egypt to Scotland – Pabasa's and another, in which the duke himself was eventually buried.

Sarcophagus of Hapmen

c. 664–525 BCE

Granite • Height: 1.2 m (3 ft), width: 1.4 m (4 ⅝ ft), length: 2.7 m (8 ⅞ ft) • From Ibn Tulun Mosque, Cairo, Egypt

BRITISH MUSEUM, LONDON, UK

This massive stone container is typical of Late period sarcophagi, making it well suited for its eventual reuse as a ritual bath tub in the Ibn Tulun Mosque – even having a 'plug hole' drilled in the base to allow water to drain out. Of chief interest is that the decoration closely replicates that on the sarcophagus of Tuthmose III, who lived almost a millennium before Hapmen. This implies either that Late period artisans had access to the king's tomb in the Valley of the Kings or that an intermediary 'pattern book' of designs had existed.

Coffin for King Menkaure

c. 664–525 BCE

Wood, traces of plaster and paint • Length: 1.6 m (5 ¼ ft) • From Giza, Egypt

BRITISH MUSEUM, LONDON, UK

The pyramids of Giza were built as secure royal tombs, but were likely to have been robbed soon after they were sealed. This coffin was discovered in 1837 by Colonel Richard Howard Vyse, who used dynamite to blast his way into Menkaure's pyramid. At first it was believed that this represented the original burial of the king. However, the shape of the coffin and the form of the inscriptions on it show that it dates to the Twenty-sixth Dynasty. This was evidently a respectful reburial of whatever were believed to be the mortal remains of King Menkaure within his own (already looted) pyramid.

Carian stela

c. 664–404 BCE

Limestone • Height: 63 cm (24 ¾ in.),
width: 31 cm (12 ¼ in.), depth: 10 cm
(3 ⅞ in.) • From Saqqara, Egypt

BRITISH MUSEUM, LONDON, UK

During the Late period, the capital
city of Memphis was home to a
multicultural community. Carians,
from western Anatolia, came
to Egypt to serve as mercenary
fighters in the Egyptian army. This
is a particularly unusual example
of a Carian-type stela, often with
Carian script as here, found at
Saqqara. The Egyptian deities
Osiris, Isis, Apis and Thoth appear
in somewhat unconventional
form. The bottom register shows
an entirely un-Egyptian scene that
betrays a Greek artistic influence:
a deceased woman, clothed in her
finery, laying on a bed attended
by male and female mourners.

Coffin of Djedbastetiuefankh

c. 400–30 BCE
Wood and paint • Length: 1.7 m (5 ⅝ ft)
From El-Hibeh, Egypt
ROEMER-UND PELIZAEUS-MUSEUM,
HILDESHEIM, GERMANY

The process of mummification was a closely guarded secret, and depictions of it are very rare. This is one of a small number of coffins from a regional cemetery in Middle Egypt that break the rules, and show some of the stages in the transformation of the corpse into a mummy. From bottom to top: the body is washed and sprinkled with natron – a sodium-based dehydrating agent; a group of embalmers, led by the jackal-headed (masked?) Anubis, approach the body; the wrapped mummy is tended by Anubis and offerings are presented.

Ptah-Sokar-Osiris figure

c. 300–30 BCE
*Wood, gold and paint • Height: 47 cm
(18 ½ in.), width of base: 34 cm
(13 ⅜ in.), depth: 16 cm (6 ¼ in.)
From Assyut, Egypt*

EGYPTIAN MUSEUM, TURIN, ITALY

The composite deity Ptah-Sokar-Osiris most often appeared as a statuette in elite burials from the end of the New Kingdom to the Late period. Figurines are usually mummiform in shape and depict the god wearing, as here, the tall plumed crown with ram's horns. Earlier statuettes mostly take the form of Osiris and were often hollow to contain rolled-up *Book of the Dead* papyri. Later versions, like this, often have hollows in the base, to hold mummified material or papyrus, and have a crouching falcon figurine.

Shabti of Horudja

c. 380–343 BCE
Faience • Height: 21.9 cm (8 ⅝ in.), width: 6.2 cm (2 ½ in.)
From Hawara, Egypt

MANCHESTER MUSEUM, UK

In an account worthy of Indiana Jones, the
archaeologist W. M. Flinders Petrie describes his
clearance of the tomb of Horudja: stripped to the
waist in order to wade through acrid water, 'while
skulls bobbed on the waves'. Petrie managed to extract
no fewer than 400 shabti figurines from around the
sarcophagus of Horudja, who was a priest of the
goddess Neith. The shabtis are fine examples of Late
period manufacture, made from at least seventeen
different moulds with individual finishing. A number
of amulets survived the waterlogged conditions in the
tomb, although most organic material was destroyed.

Sarcophagus lid of Ptahhotep

525–500 BCE
Greywacke • Height: 2.1 m (6 ⅞ ft), width: 82.5 cm (32 ½ in.)
From Giza, Egypt

ASHMOLEAN MUSEUM, OXFORD, UK

Discovered in a deep shaft burial known as 'Campbell's Tomb' at Giza, this sarcophagus is typical of contemporary anthropoid (human-shaped) examples. These display a wide 'smile' across a disproportionately large face, which seem rather un-Egyptian. The hieroglyphic inscription of Chapter 72 of the *Book of the Dead* assures us of its serious, regenerative intention. The owner, Ptahhotep, was a treasury official who served in the reign of Darius I, dating him to the Persian period.

Stela of Taimhotep

42 BCE

*Limestone • Height: 90.2 cm
(35 ½ in.), width: 44.2 cm (17 ⅜ in.)
From Saqqara, Egypt*

BRITISH MUSEUM, LONDON, UK

It was very unusual for the Egyptians to make a direct reference to death; however, the text of this stela contains an evocative speech by a woman called Taimhotep from beyond the grave. She laments the condition of death and urges her husband to live life to the full. Perhaps he commissioned the monument to assuage a feeling of guilt. The stela is dated precisely to within the reign of Cleopatra VII and – intriguingly – states that it was erected near the tomb of the deified sage Imhotep, which is still unlocated.

Rome in Egypt

Egypt's Roman rulers, like the Ptolemies before them, respected pharaonic traditions and had themselves depicted performing rituals for the Egyptian pantheon. Here, Emperor Trajan (98–117 CE) presents ritual objects to the goddess Hathor outside her temple at Dendera.

The defeat of Mark Antony and Cleopatra at the Battle of Actium in 31 BCE marks a distinct turning point in the history of Egypt. Although often romanticized, Cleopatra's attempts to secure self-determination for her country were serious – only to be foiled by Octavian, who went on to become Emperor Augustus.

Following on in a well-established pattern, Augustus and the later emperors after him had themselves depicted in the mould of pharaohs: pious Egyptian monarchs shown on temple walls making offerings to the gods and performing rituals. Like the Ptolemies before them, the Caesars made diplomatic efforts to maintain good relations with temple priesthoods – the physical and intellectual bastions of pharaonic traditions – and supported continued construction work. Despite the fact that most Roman emperors rarely spent any time in Egypt, many tourists to Greco-Roman temples today find their images indistinguishable from those of earlier kings.

Rome had more of a special relationship with Egypt than with other provinces. Although Egypt was heavily

Egypt exerted a particular fascination over the Romans. This Nilotic landscape was painted near Rome in about 100 BCE. It depicts Egypt from Ethiopia to the Mediterranean, and emphasizes the importance of the river for life along its banks. Pharaonic temples coexist with classical-style structures, amid various forms of wildlife and vegetation.

taxed as the so-called 'granary of the Empire', it was also seen as a mysterious land of ancient and secret wisdom by both the Romans and the Greeks before them. The cultural importance of Egypt to the Romans is illustrated by the number of pharaonic monuments that were physically transported to Rome – not an easy endeavour, especially in view of the sea-crossing required. Indeed, Rome today boasts more standing obelisks than in all of Egypt. Emperor Hadrian seems to have been a particular Egyptophile, collecting both pharaonic and Egyptianizing sculpture for his villa at Tivoli, and even deifying his lover Antinous, who drowned in the Nile, as a quasi-Egyptian god.

Unique insights into preparations for death and expectations for the afterlife come from the Roman cemetery of Hawara, near the Faiyum lake. Here, the Middle Kingdom king Amenemhat III was still revered as a god in the first centuries CE. Not far from his pyramid a huge number of Roman mummies was discovered by the British archaeologist William Matthew Flinders Petrie. The practice of mummification continued well into the

Roman period in Egypt, although cremation also seems to have been practised. Petrie's discovery of dozens of painted mummy portraits at Hawara led to the term 'Faiyum Portraits' being applied to the whole group, known from different sites in Roman Egypt. These striking encaustic paintings were created using a mixture of pigment and hot wax and are often haunting in their intensity. Petrie found evidence at Hawara that these images may have been hung on walls before being cut down to be included over the face of the deceased, often inserted in elaborately patterned bindings. Sometimes, the bandages of the mummy carry traditional pharaonic funerary iconography in addition to the fashionable Roman appearance of the upper body, implying the Romans were hedging their bets about who they might meet in the afterlife. Very few objects seem to have been buried with mummies, which seem to have been stored in the houses of the living before being interred communally.

Details of the portraits show that some of the men depicted were soldiers, bearing out the fact that some Roman soldiers would have been pensioned off to Egypt after their active service had come to an end. Details of life in Roman Egypt, including instances of civil unrest, are known from papyrus documents. Petrie found papyri of many sorts at Hawara, including parts of literary works such as Homer's *Iliad*; he even unwrapped mummified crocodiles in the hope that he would find other examples of documents. Similarly, the site of Oxyrhynchus in Middle Egypt yielded a huge quantity of papyri that can be used to reconstruct life in Roman Egypt. The discovery of the site of Karanis near the Faiyum provided both papyri and has complemented the texts with important surviving settlement architecture.

The end of Roman rule, in 394 CE, coincided with the last known hieroglyphic inscription, at the temple of Isis at Philae. By this time Egypt had largely become Christianized, bringing to an end millennia of worship of many gods. Despite this, many pharaonic social practices survived the demise of paganism and continued into the Islamic era.

The continued practice of mummification in Roman Egypt combined traditional materials and techniques, but represented the deceased in ways different to those of pharaonic times. The dead are shown in painted portraits as they would have wished to look during life. Gold was still employed by those who could afford it.

TOY HORSE

c. 100 BCE–300 CE
Wood • Height: 11.5 cm (4 ½ in.), length: 15.7 cm (6 ⅛ in.)
From Gurob, Egypt
MANCHESTER MUSEUM, UK

Very few objects from antiquity can be identified with certainty
as children's toys. Modern conceptions of childhood influence
our interpretations of objects that may seem crude or childlike,
but these impressions may be misleading. An unknown
religious or ritual use, even for seemingly unsophisticated
objects, cannot be discounted.

Several finds from Roman period settlements in the
Faiyum region are significant because they come from places
where individuals lived, rather than died or went to worship,
thus giving some indication of 'everyday life'. This relatively
crude horse is one of several known that have no obvious
religious function, but whose movability suggests intended
use. A hole has been pierced through the neck where a
string or cord could have been attached to pull the toy
along on its wheels. The wheels are held in place on the
axles by wooden dowels. On its right side, the horse has
three sets of incised lines, perhaps to imitate the ribcage
of the animal as it appeared in life. Horses may have been
connected particularly with warfare and military activity, or
may specifically have been related to the tale of the Trojan
Horse, well known in contemporary Roman society.

Horses were known in Egypt from the New Kingdom onwards and were frequently associated in monumental reliefs with warfare or the military.

Writing board

c. 100 BCE–300 CE
*Wood • Length: 14.5 cm
(5 ¾ in.), width: 7.5 cm (3 in.)
From Oxyrhynchus, Egypt*

MANCHESTER MUSEUM, UK

As in pharaonic times, very few people in Roman-period Egypt were able to write. This wooden board is evidence for the practice of writing, and perhaps also for teaching. It has a shallow depression that would have been filled with wax, traces of which remain. Text would be impressed into the wax using a stylus and could then be easily erased or corrected. Holes imply that it had a wooden cover to protect whatever was written within. At the site of Oxyrhynchus a major deposit of Greco-Roman papyri was found, some of which might have been drafted using this writing board.

Snake bracelet

c. 100 BCE–200 CE
Gold • Diameter: 7.2 cm (2 ⅞ in.)
From Egypt
GETTY MUSEUM,
LOS ANGELES, USA

The modern image of Cleopatra as the glamorous figure portrayed by the actress Elizabeth Taylor was influenced by ancient jewelry such as this. Similar bangles were depicted on mummy mask coverings of women; the serpent was a symbol of royal power and protection. The dangerous aspect of the snake could be harnessed to overcome evil, and it was believed to spit fire and poison at enemies of the pharaoh. Such royal prerogatives were adopted in the funerary customs of non-royals in the late Ptolemaic and Roman periods because of their perceived effectiveness.

Hoop earrings

c. 100 BCE–200 CE

Gold • Height: 2.1 cm (⅞ in.), width: 1.8 cm (¾ in.), depth: 1 cm (⅜ in.) • From Egypt

GETTY MUSEUM, LOS ANGELES, USA

Although there is some evidence for men wearing earrings in pharaonic Egypt, notably kings in the New Kingdom, by the Roman period only women are depicted wearing them. These hoop earrings terminate in antelope heads, a motif common in the Near East. Each hoop is comprised of a length of cable around which wire was coiled. The antelope's eyes may once have been inlaid. Similar hoop earrings appear in Roman-period painted mummy portraits and cartonnage masks of women from Hawara and other Faiyum cemeteries.

Garment

c. 300 – 400 CE

*Linen and wool • Height: 1.7 m
(5 ⅝ ft), width: 1.4 m (4 ⅝ ft)
From Akhmim, Egypt*

METROPOLITAN MUSEUM
OF ART, NEW YORK CITY, USA

The survival of clothing, particularly from the Roman period, is largely due to the fact that the dead were buried dressed in their finest garments. No attempt seems to have been made to embalm the corpse, and the associated human remains in burials were frequently discarded by excavators in favour of keeping the textiles. This garment is too long even for an adult wearer – the conspicuous consumption of expensive fabric was perhaps a sign of status. It is decorated with bands called clavi, composed of vine leaves and interlacing patterns, and dancing warriors decorate the squares. Such pagan themes were soon to be replaced with Christian imagery.

Sprang cap

c. 400 – 600 CE
*Wool • Height: 42 cm (16½ in.),
width: 28 cm (11 in.)
From Lahun, Egypt*

WHITWORTH ART GALLERY,
MANCHESTER, UK

In Christian Egypt, it was common to bury the deceased fully dressed. A popular item worn by women in late antiquity was a cap or head-covering. These may have functioned something like a hairnet, and are often of very brightly coloured wool or linen in either a rectangular (as here) or conical shape. The method employed has been much debated but most agree that it is a technique called sprang – a type of knotting (rather than knitting) – that produces a stretchy fabric well suited to coverings for the hair.

Silver bust of Serapis

c. 100 – 200 CE
Silver • Height: 15.6 cm (6 ⅛ in.), diameter: 9.5 cm (3 ¾ in.)
From Egypt
METROPOLITAN MUSEUM OF ART, NEW YORK
CITY, USA

With the arrival of the Greek Ptolemies, a new deity
dominated the Egyptian pantheon: Serapis, a god who
combined aspects of Osiris, Apis and Dionysus. This
multicultural deity appealed to both Egyptians and
Greeks. He is recognizable as a bearded man with long
curly hair and a grain measure atop his head, although
it is missing here. The worship of Serapis became
popular during the Roman period in Egypt. His major
cult centre was located at the Serapeum of Alexandria
until it was destroyed by Christians in about 389 CE.

Bust of an emperor

c. 14 – 20 CE

*Green basanite • Height: 47 cm (18 ½ in.), width: 30 cm
(11 ¾ in.), depth: 24 cm (9 ½ in.) From Egypt*

BRITISH MUSEUM, LONDON, UK

This striking bust probably represents Emperor
Germanicus, who visited Egypt shortly before he died
in Antioch in 19 CE. Many standing pharaonic and
Roman monuments were later 'Christianized' by the
addition of a cross. Here, the emperor's visage has
been deliberately mutilated rather than accidentally
damaged; hacking has occurred on the nose, right ear
and neck, and a cross has been incised on the forehead,
almost in an attempt to exorcize the pagan image.
These actions may not have been contemporary with
one another.

Horus as a Roman soldier

c. 1 – 200 CE
Limestone • Height: 54.5 cm (21 ½ in.), width: 31.8 cm (12 ½ in.), depth: 25.8 cm (10 ⅛ in.) From Egypt

BRITISH MUSEUM, LONDON, UK

A number of Egyptian gods were represented in non-Egyptian attire during the Roman period, presenting them in a way that appealed to people from different cultures. The falcon-headed god Horus had always had an association with victory and military triumph, so it may seem natural that he should appear in the attire of a Roman soldier. Here he is represented seated with his legs casually spread in the manner of a senior Greco-Roman deity. The falcon's face is strikingly lifelike, and the scale armour of the upper body echoes a falcon's feathers.

Phallus flask

c. 100 – 200 CE
Glass • Length: 10 cm (3 ⅞ in.), width: 3.2 cm (1 ¼ in.) • From Hawara, Egypt
PETRIE MUSEUM OF EGYPTIAN
ARCHAEOLOGY, LONDON, UK

Glass blowing was a well-known technique in Roman Egypt, and a significant quantity of glass vessels have survived from Roman period contexts in the Faiyum region. Gods such as Min, Bes and Osiris were associated with fertility rituals, often involving phallic imagery, in pharaonic times and later. This example of a bottle in the shape of a phallus was found in the grave of a young woman at Hawara, alongside other erotic or fertility symbols. The intention of the phallus was thus to promote rebirth in the afterlife.

Statue of Antinous

c. 131–138 CE
Marble • Height: 2.4 m (7 ⅞ ft), width: 77 cm
(30 ⅜ in.), depth: 79 cm (31 ⅛ in.)
From Hadrian's Villa, Tivoli, Italy

VATICAN MUSEUMS, ROME, ITALY

Antinous was the young lover of Emperor
Hadrian (117–138 CE). Following Antinous's
sudden death by drowning in the Nile in
130 CE, the emperor founded the city of
Antinopolis nearby. The fate of Antinous
was likened to the death of the drowned god
Osiris, and he was deified as Osiris-Antinous.
Here he is shown with a pharaonic *nemes*-
headdress and *shendyt* kilt. The cult spread
rapidly across the empire, especially during
the final years of Hadrian's reign. Around
one hundred ancient images of Antinous are
known, although the iconic status of the 'gay
god' has appealed to modernity and inspired
countless further representations.

Osiris-in-Hydria jar

c. 0 – 100 CE

*Bronze • Height: 9.2 cm (3 ⅝ in.), width: 3.9 cm
(1 ½ in.) • From Egypt*

ISRAEL MUSEUM, JERUSALEM, ISRAEL

The god Osiris was associated with the
provision of refreshment in the afterlife.
Roman-period jars topped with human
heads are often called Osiris-in-Hydria
vessels. The original function of the jar
was as a ritual libation pitcher, with the
distinctive but conflated Egyptian elements
of the tripartite wig, uraeus cobra, long beard
and tall feathered crown. The association of
these vessels with the area of Canopus in the
Nile Delta led to the alternative term 'Osiris
Canopus' vessels. From this association arose
the term 'canopic jar' as a designation for the
earlier containers for the preserved internal
organs, with human or animal heads.

Statue of Anubis

c. 100–138 CE

Marble • Height: 1.5 m (4 ⅞ ft),
width: 50 cm (19 ⅝ in.) • From Tivoli,
Rome, Italy

VATICAN MUSEUMS, ROME, ITALY

The jackal-headed god Anubis was, for the Romans, a particularly distinctive member of the hybrid animal-human Egyptian pantheon. Some Romans derided the concept of such composite deities. The poet Juvenal mockingly asked: 'who knows not what monsters demented Egypt worships?' Here, Anubis is provided with a sun disc atop his head, a Greco-Roman embellishment in depictions of the god. He is, however, in Roman attire with the attributes of Mercury, with whom he was identified. This statue comes from Hadrian's villa at Tivoli, where it was displayed alongside a number of genuinely ancient Egyptian pieces.

Sundial amulet

100 BCE–200 CE

Wood • Length: 9.8 cm (3 ⅞ in.) • From
Meroë, Sudan

GARSTANG MUSEUM OF ARCHAEOLOGY, LIVERPOOL, UK

This object takes the form of a temple pylon, with the details of winged sun discs above the gateway. While such pylons are well known as the frontages of pharaonic temples, this feature was widely imitated in Meroitic architecture. The semicircle beneath the pylon takes the form of a 'sundial', known from the New Kingdom onwards. This example is divided into eleven sections, rather than the usual twelve, used to represent the twelve hours of the day and night respectively. This piece is probably amuletic rather than practical, though its exact meaning is unclear.

267

Mummy tag

30 BCE–395 CE
*Wood and ink • Height: 10.2 cm
(4 in.), width: 6.2 cm (2 ½ in.),
depth: 1.2 cm (½ in.) • Most likely
from Dongala, Sudan*

BROOKLYN MUSEUM, NEW YORK
CITY, USA

In the Roman period, changes in funerary preparations meant that the name of the deceased did not usually appear on the decoration of a mummified body. As a result, the practice of identifying mummies with wooden tags became common. This was both practical and provided magical identification for eternity.
This example is written in both Greek and Demotic Egyptian scripts. In Greek the deceased is recorded as 'Horus, son of Psenmonthes, stonecutter'. The more extensive Demotic text gives the name of the deceased: 'Horus, son of Psenmonth' and his functions 'the stonecutter and priest of Imhotep'.

Cinerary urn

c. 0–200 CE
*Faience • Height: 23.1 cm (9 ⅛ in.),
diameter (mouth): 19 cm (7 ½ in.)
From Egypt*

DETROIT INSTITUTE OF ARTS, USA

The idea of burning the body was anathema to the ancient Egyptians, yet cremation was common in Roman funerary practice. The custom was imported into Egypt by the Romans, about the same time the traditional form of mummification was still being practised. Glazed receptacles such as this were used for the ashes. This example shows an unusual spiralled decoration perhaps in imitation of glass. Roman glazeworks are particularly well known from kilns and waste deposits at an area of Memphis called Kom Helul, and this may be from where this vessel derives.

Funerary wreath

c. 100 – 200 CE

*Plant material • Height: 35 cm
(13 ¾ in.), width: 25 cm (9 ⅞ in.)
From Hawara, Egypt*

BRITISH MUSEUM, LONDON, UK

The growth of plants and flowers had a strong connotation of rebirth for the ancient Egyptians and this continued in the Roman period. Very appropriately, this carefully tied garland is created with a species known as *immortelles* (*Helichrysum stoechas*), native to Italy and Greece, and may have been known as an 'everlasting' flower in ancient times as it is today. Very similar wreaths, usually painted pink, are often represented being grasped by the deceased in cartonnage mummy coverings. Ephemeral floral remains survived with many Greco-Roman mummies, indicating their significance during funeral rituals.

Funerary mask

c. 100 – 120 CE

*Plaster, linen and paint • Height: 68 cm
(26 ¾ in.), width: 39 cm (15 ⅜ in.) • Most
likely from Meir, Egypt*

BRITISH MUSEUM, LONDON, UK

Such plaster masks were popular among the elite of Middle Egypt. This example is very similar to a group from Meir that may derive from the same workshop. Although not a portrait, the mask nonetheless has a bright, lifelike appearance. The woman is represented as if lying flat upon her bier. She wears a floral garland in her hair. Her jewelry consists of a winged scarab, and she is flanked by pharaonic funerary deities. Her exposed breasts emphasize gender identity and sexuality as a catalyst for rebirth.

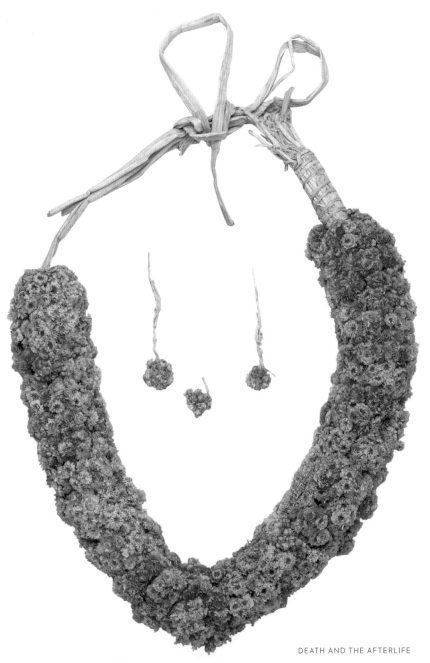

DOUBLE-SIDED MUMMY PORTRAIT

c. 110–120 CE

Wood and paint • Height: 41 cm (16⅛ in.), width: 32.5 cm (12¾ in.) • From Hawara, Egypt

MANCHESTER MUSEUM, UK

Mummification continued to be practised in Egypt for the elite well into the Roman period. Greater care was taken of the outer appearance of the mummy than the inside, as CT-scans reveal evisceration was rare. Rather than mummy masks depicting a perfect, generic image of the deceased, some Roman period mummies are provided with painted portraits following Roman traditions for representing the human face – although these may still represent idealized visions of the deceased.

This double-sided image shows a finished portrait of a man (top), and a rougher (partially erased?) sketch (bottom) on the reverse perhaps representing the same individual. The hairstyles on both portraits suggest a date between the reigns of Trajan and Hadrian. The portrait was discovered, along with hundreds of others, affixed to a mummy at a major Roman-period necropolis at Hawara, near the Faiyum lake. Although only a small proportion of mummies were provided with portraits, those which survived were of high quality and acquired the name 'Faiyum Portraits'. There is circumstantial evidence that a display of Faiyum Portraits, on view at the Egyptian Hall in Piccadilly, London, in the late 1880s, was seen by the writer Oscar Wilde and may have inspired his novel *The Picture of Dorian Gray* (1890).

The pyramid of Amenemhat III looms over the landscape at Hawara, and may have attracted the burials of Roman period individuals who wished to be associated with the ancient king venerated as a god.

Mummy portrait of a youth

c. 150 – 200 CE

*Wood and paint • Height: 20.3 cm
(8 in.), width: 13 cm (5 ⅛ in.)
Most likely from Hawara, Egypt*

GETTY VILLA, MALIBU, USA

The child depicted in this portrait has the traditional side-lock of youth in which he wears a golden pin. Such a hairstyle was worn by both sexes in the Roman period to show an association with the cult of the goddess Isis. This nameless boy is unusual in also having two tufts of hair which may be the result of ritual shaving to ward off serious illness, although the existence of the portrait indicates that this was in vain. His tunic has a narrow purple band (*clavus*), which indicates the wealth of his parents, who could afford to have such a mummy portrait painted.

A coffin for two brothers

c. 175 – 200 CE
*Wood and paint • Length: 1.2 m
(3 ⅞ ft), width: 55 cm (21 ⅝ in.)
From Thebes, Egypt*

NATIONAL MUSEUMS
SCOTLAND, EDINBURGH, UK

This unique double coffin was
prepared for the interment of
two young boys, Petamun and
Penhorpabik. The gold-leaf-
covered mummies of the boys were
found inside, perhaps the victims
of the same disease. Although
their relationship is not stated, it is
likely that they were half-brothers
with the same father. The names of
their different mothers appear in the
inscriptions. On the lid, the boys are
shown as divine, with royal sceptres.
On the base of the trough, two figures of
the goddess Nut offer protection to each
boy. She wears Roman dress but with a
hieroglyph of her name above her head.

Glossary

Akh Spiritual influence of the blessed deceased; the aspect most like the term 'ghost'.

Amarna Modern name of the city founded by King Akhenaten, often used to describe his reign in general.

Amulet Protective object worn by the living and/or provided for the dead.

Amun Theban god who became chief Egyptian deity from *c.* 1500 BCE onwards.

Ankh Looped cross hieroglyphic symbol for 'life'.

Anubis Jackal(-headed) god of the necropolis, who played a key part in mummification.

Apis Sacred bull believed to be a living form of the Memphite god Ptah.

Aten God promoted almost exclusively by King Akhenaten, visualized as a sun disc with rays ending in hands.

Ba The spirit of movement of the deceased, visualized as a human-headed bird that could leave the tomb.

Barque Sacred boat used to transport a divine or royal statue.

Book of the Dead Funerary text consisting of a collection of spells intended to act as the deceased's passport to and guidebook within the afterlife.

Canopic jar One of a set of four vessels to safeguard the mummified internal organs of the deceased that would be needed in the afterlife, with human or animal-shaped lids.

Cartonnage Material composed of layers of linen or papyrus and plaster.

Cartouche Ring drawn around the name of the king, and often the queen, to provide magical protection to the named individual.

Cippus Statue or amulet with texts of healing power usually depicting the god Horus.

Deir el-Bahri Area famed for the temples of King Montuhotep II and Queen Hatshepsut, intensively reused for tombs in the Third Intermediate and Late periods.

Deir el-Medina Town built to house workers employed by the state to quarry and decorate royal tombs in the Valley of the Kings, reused in Roman period as a cemetery.

Encaustic Painting technique that combined pigment with hot wax to produce lifelike portraits in the Roman period.

Faience Glazed ceramic made by firing a mix of clay, quartz and a colouring agent (usually a copper compound) to produce a distinctive blue.

God's Wife Religious title held by some royal women, connected to the cult of Amun.

Heb-sed Ritual festival or 'jubilee' that celebrated the the rule of a pharaoh after thirty years on the throne.

Hieratic Cursive version of the hieroglyphic script used for correspondence and other documents.

Hieroglyphic Monumental script of pictorial signs used for official inscriptions.

Ibis A long-legged wading bird sacred to the god of wisdom and writing, Thoth.

Ka The spirit of sustenance of the deceased, conceptualized as a double or twin that dwelled in images of the deceased in the tomb and temple(s).

Kush Area to the south of Egypt, in northern modern Sudan; home of the Twenty-fifth Dynasty of rulers.

Mastaba A monumental tomb, usually of Old or Middle Kingdom date, from the Arabic word for 'bench'.

Memphis/Memphite Principal residence of the king and seat of government throughout most of the pharaonic period.

Mummiform Human figure in the shape of a wrapped mummy, used to depict the dead and the gods.

Natron Sodium compound used to dehydrate the body during mummification.

Nemes Distinctive striped headcloth, worn exclusively by the pharaoh.

Nubia General area to the south of Egypt, derived from the term for 'gold'.

Osiris God of rebirth and major deity of the Egyptian pantheon throughout pharaonic times.

Ostracon Flake of limestone or potsherd used as a surface for writing or drawing.

Papyrus Paperlike substance used for writing, made from overlaid strips of papyrus plant stalks.

Pectoral Chest ornament worn around the neck.

Pharaoh Title of the king of Egypt from the New Kingdom onwards, derived from the Egyptian term for 'great house' or 'palace'.

Ramesseum Temple dedicated to the cult of King Ramesses II on the west bank of Thebes.

Sarcophagus Stone container for the body and/or coffin(s) of the deceased.

Scarab Dung-beetle (*Scarabaeus sacer*) sacred to the Egyptians, associated with regeneration and rebirth.

Serdab Closed chamber in a tomb made to hold a statue or statues of the deceased.

Shabti Servant figurine in the form of a mummy, provided with tools to undertake agricultural tasks for the deceased in the afterlife.

Stela An inscribed tablet made of stone or wood, usually to commemorate an individual, event or statement.

Uraeus Representation of one or more cobras, worn on the brow of kings, queens or deities.

Valley of the Kings The royal necropolis in Thebes between *c.* 1500 and 1100 BCE.

Wedjat The 'Eye of Horus', a symbol of completeness, healing and protection.

Index

*Page numbers in **bold** refer to illustrations*

Museum Index

Picture Credits

All works are courtesy of the museums listed in the individual captions.

12 Ashmolean Museum, University of Oxford, UK/Bridgeman Images 14 Peter Horree/Alamy Stock Photo 15 Mike P Shepherd/Alamy Stock Photo 17 UC28614B1 © the Petrie Museum, UCL Culture, University College London 18 Photo by Jeremy Jowell/Majority World/UIG via Getty Images 18-19 Manchester Museum, University of Manchester 20 Manchester Museum, University of Manchester 21 Museum of Fine Arts, Boston, Massachusetts, USA/Emily Esther Sears Fund/Bridgeman Images 22 © Michael C. Carlos Museum, Emory University. Photo by Bruce M. White, 2008 23 © 2017. Museum of Fine Arts, Boston. All rights reserved/Scala, Florence 24 © The Trustees of the British Museum 25 Courtesy of the Oriental Institute of the University of Chicago 26 Manchester Museum, University of Manchester 27 Ashmolean Museum, University of Oxford, UK/Bridgeman Images 28 Photo by Werner Forman/Universal Images Group/Getty Images 29 Photo by Werner Forman/Universal Images Group/Getty Images 30 Photo by Werner Forman/Universal Images Group/Getty Images 31 © The Trustees of the British Museum 32 Photo © Musée du Louvre, Dist. RMN-Grand Palais/Georges Poncet 33 Brooklyn Museum of Art, New York, USA/Charles Edwin Wilbour Fund/Bridgeman Images 34 Fitzwilliam Museum, University of Cambridge, UK/Bridgeman Images 35 Photo: Juergen Liepe © 2017. Photo Scala, Florence/bpk, Bildagentur fuer Kunst, Kultur und Geschichte, Berlin 36 Ashmolean Museum, University of Oxford, UK/Bridgeman Images 37 Ashmolean Museum, University of Oxford, UK/Bridgeman Images 38 National Museum of Antiquities, Leiden 39 World Museum, National Museums Liverpool/Bridgeman Images 40-41 The Metropolitan Museum of Art, New York/Rogers Fund, 1919 41 Photo by Xavier ROSSI/Gamma-Rapho via Getty Images 43 © 2017. Photo Scala, Florence/bpk, Bildagentur fuer Kunst, Kultur und Geschichte, Berlin 44 Photo by DEA/G. DAGLI ORTI/De Agostini/Getty Images 46 Photo by DEA/G. DAGLI ORTI/De Agostini/Getty Images 47 Photo By DEA/A. JEMOLO/De Agostini/Getty Images 48 Museum of Fine Arts, Boston, Massachusetts, USA/Harvard University - Museum of Fine Arts Expedition/Bridgeman Images 49 Photo by DEA/A. JEMOLO/De Agostini/Getty Images 50 © 2017. Photo Scala, Florence/FMAE, Torino 51 © 2017. Museum of Fine Arts, Boston. All rights reserved/Scala, Florence 52 Photo by Prisma/UIG via Getty Images 53 Photo by DEA/G. DAGLI ORTI/De Agostini/Getty Images 54-55 © 2017. DeAgostini Picture Library/Scala, Florence 56 Egyptian National Museum, Cairo, Egypt/Bridgeman Images 58 Brooklyn Museum of Art, New York, USA/Charles Edwin Wilbour Fund/Bridgeman Images 59 Photo by Christophel Fine Art/UIG via Getty Images 60 Brooklyn Museum of Art, New York, USA/Bridgeman Images 61 The Metropolitan Museum of Art, New York/Rogers Fund, 1926 62 Photo by Werner Forman/Universal Images Group/Getty Images 63 Courtesy of the Oriental Institute of the University of Chicago 64 Photo © RMN-Grand Palais (musée du Louvre)/Hervé Lewandowski 65 Courtesy of the Oriental Institute of the University of Chicago 66 Photo by De Agostini/A. Dagli Orti/Getty Images 67 Museum of Fine Arts, Boston, Massachusetts, USA/Harvard University - Museum of Fine Arts Expedition/Bridgeman Images 68 © The Trustees of the British Museum 69 © 2017. Museum of Fine Arts, Boston. All rights reserved/Scala, Florence 70 © The Trustees of the British Museum 71 Museum of Fine Arts, Boston, Massachusetts, USA/Purchased by A. M. Lythgoe/Bridgeman Images 72 Photo by Werner Forman/Universal Images Group/Getty Images 74 Mark Davidson/Alamy Stock Photo 75 Photo by Leemage/Corbis via Getty Images 76 Manchester Museum, University of Manchester 78-79 Manchester Museum, University of Manchester 80-81 Manchester Museum, University of Manchester 83 The Metropolitan Museum of Art, New York/Purchase, Edward S. Harkness Gift, 1926 (26.7.1287a-k); Gift of Lord Carnarvon, 2012 (2012.508) 84-85 The Metropolitan Museum of Art, New York/ Purchase, Rogers Fund and Henry Walters Gift, 1916 86 © The Trustees of the British Museum 87 The Metropolitan Museum of Art, New York/ Rogers Fund, 1908 88 Glasgow Art Gallery and Museum, Scotland/Bridgeman Images 89 UC32158 © the Petrie Museum, UCL Culture, University College London 90 © The Trustees of the British Museum 91 © The Trustees of the British Museum 92 The Nelson-Atkins Museum of Art, Kansas City, Missouri. Purchase: William Rockhill Nelson Trust, 62-11. Image courtesy The Metropolitan Museum of Art, New York 93 Egyptian National Museum, Cairo, Egypt/Bridgeman Images 94 © The Trustees of the British Museum 95 Museum of Fine Arts, Boston, Massachusetts, USA/Harvard University - Museum of Fine Arts Expedition/Bridgeman Images 96-97 Antikenmuseum Basel und Sammlung Ludwig 97 The Walters Art Museum, Baltimore 99 Fitzwilliam Museum, University of Cambridge, UK/Bridgeman Images 100 Image courtesy of The Garstang Museum of Archaeology, University of Liverpool 101 Courtesy of The New York Academy of Medicine Library 102 Ashmolean Museum, University of Oxford, UK/Bridgeman Images 103 Manchester Museum, University of Manchester 104 Photo by De Agostini/W. Buss/ Getty Images 105 The Metropolitan Museum of Art, New York/Rogers Fund and Edward S. Harkness Gift, 1920 106 © 2017. Image copyright The Metropolitan Museum of Art/Art Resource/Scala, Florence 108-109 © The Trustees of the British Museum 109 © 2017. The Fitzwilliam Museum, Cambridge/Scala, Florence 110 Photo by ALESSANDRO VANNINI/Corbis via Getty Images 112 Photo by Waring Abbott/Getty Images 113 Joana Kruse/Alamy Stock Photo 114 Photo by DeAgostini/Getty Images 115 Photo © RMN-Grand Palais (musée du Louvre)/Les frères Chuzeville 116 The J. Paul Getty Museum, Los Angeles 117 World History Archive/Alamy Stock Photo 118 The Metropolitan Museum of Art, New York/Gift of Theodore M. Davis, 1910 119 Photo by DEA/G. DAGLI ORTI/De Agostini/Getty Images 120-121 Purchase, Edward S. Harkness Gift, 1926 121 Manchester Museum, University of Manchester 122 The Metropolitan Museum of Art, New York /Purchase, Edward S. Harkness Gift, 1926 123 [EG4007], Oriental Museum, Durham University 124 akg-images/Erich Lessing 125 Fitzwilliam Museum, University of Cambridge, UK/Bridgeman Images 126 World Museum, National Museums Liverpool/Bridgeman Images 127 © 2017. Museum of Fine Arts, Boston. All rights reserved/Scala, Florence 128 akg-images/Album/Asf 129 The Metropolitan Museum of Art, New York/Rogers Fund, 1929 130 © The Trustees of the British Museum 130-131 Photo: Juergen Liepe.© 2017. Photo Scala, Florence/bpk, Bildagentur fuer Kunst, Kultur und Geschichte, Berlin 132 World History Archive/Alamy Stock Photo 132-133 The Metropolitan Museum of Art, New York/Rogers Fund, 1918 134 Photo by DEA/G. SIOEN/De Agostini/Getty Images 135 Photo © RMN-Grand Palais (musée du Louvre)/René-Gabriel Ojéda 136 Photo: Olaf M.Tessmer. © 2017. Photo Scala, Florence/bpk, Bildagentur fuer Kunst, Kultur und Geschichte, Berlin 137 © 2017. Photo Scala, Florence 138-139 Prisma by Dukas Presseagentur GmbH/Alamy Stock Photo 140 Photo: Juergen Liepe. © 2017. Photo Scala, Florence/bpk, Bildagentur fuer Kunst, Kultur und Geschichte, Berlin 141 Photo by DEA/G. SIOEN/De Agostini/Getty Images 142 The Walters Art Museum, Baltimore 143 Photo by PHAS/UIG via Getty Images 144-145 World Museum, National Museums Liverpool/Bridgeman Images 145 Photo by Ed Giles/

Acknowledgments

In loving memory of Joyce Price and Tracey Rodger.
I am grateful to Elspeth Beidas at Quintessence for approaching me about the 'Pocket Museum' project, and to Hannah Phillips and Kate Duncan for their forbearance during the production stages. David Michael Smith was generous with practical advice; individual selections and comments arose out of discussions with many colleagues and friends. Finally, as always, I offer heartfelt thanks to David Joseph Roper for all his support.

Front cover: Statuette of Amun, c. 945–715 BCE, *The Metropolitan Museum of Art, New York/Purchase, Edward S. Harkness Gift, 1926*

Back cover: Ibis bird coffin, c. 664–30 BCE, *Glasgow Art Gallery and Museum, Scotland/Bridgeman Images*

Page 2: Statue of Padiaset, c. 1850–1750 BCE, *The Walters Art Museum, Baltimore*

First published in the United Kingdom in 2018 by
Thames & Hudson Ltd, 181A High Holborn,
London WC1V 7QX

© 2018 Quarto Publishing plc

This book was designed and produced by
Quintessence Editions, an imprint of The Quarto Group
The Old Brewery, 6 Blundell Street, London N7 9BH

Project Editor	Hannah Phillips
Designer	Josse Pickard
Editor	Fiona Plowman
Picture Researcher	Kate Duncan
Production Manager	Anna Pauletti
Editorial Director	Ruth Patrick
Publisher	Philip Cooper

British Library Cataloguing-in-Publication Data
A catalogue record for this book is available from the British Library

ISBN 978-0-500-51984-4

Printed and bound in China

To find out about all our publications, please visit **www.thamesandhudson.com**.
There you can subscribe to our e-newsletter, browse or download our current
catalogue, and buy any titles that are in print.